PRAYER AND MODERN MAN

Apocalypse: The Book of Revelation
The Betrayal of the West
False Presence of the Kingdom
Hope in Time of Abandonment
The New Demons
The Presence of the Kingdom
The Theological Foundation of Law
Violence

JACQUES ELLUL

Prayer and Modern Man

Translated by C. Edward Hopkin

A Crossroad Book
THE SEABURY PRESS • NEW YORK

1979
The Seabury Press
815 Second Avenue
New York, N.Y. 10017

Copyright © 1970 by Jacques Ellul. All rights reserved. No part of this book may be reproduced, stored in a retrieval system, or transmitted in any form or by any means, electronic, mechanical, photocopying, recording, or otherwise, without the written permission of The Seabury Press.

Fifth Printing
First *Seabury Paperback* edition 1973

Printed in the United States of America

Library of Congress Catalog Card Number: 79-103845
ISBN: 0-8164-2081-5

PREFACE

This is not a book of piety. The reader will not find recommendations or advice about how to pray well, or any examples. I am not trying to guide him in his prayer, or provide him with a prayer book. I am too deeply convinced that prayer is an act involving the whole person, a decision which is profoundly individual. Hence it is not for me to direct and influence the reader.

Furthermore, I fail to see what good is done by those model prayers (we already have one model which embraces them all), and still less those technical directions concerning the appropriate times for prayer, the establishing of interior silence, or the breathing rhythm which facilitates prayer. If prayer is not the deepest and the most completely free cry from the heart it seems to me to be indecent; and it must have those little technical devices—one discovers them for himself, adapts them to himself, as the expression of his own prayer, of his own real need to pray. Otherwise they are nothing but a false appearance and a parody. If the need to pray is not present, then all the models and procedures are useless.

A prayer book presupposes that the person to whom it is addressed wants to pray, already knows how to pray, and that prayer is a part of his life. In that case, yes—for that committed person it can be useful to provide him with better opportunities and expressions for prayer. But today we no longer are faced with the person who is already won over, convinced, the stuttering Christian who needs to be taught to speak yet a Christian notwithstanding. That person belonging to a Christian society no longer exists. The man of our times does not know how to pray; but much more than that, he has neither the desire nor the need to do so. He does not find the deep source of prayer within himself. I am acquainted with this man. I know him well. It is I myself.

Am I, then, to write a book of apologetics to demonstrate that prayer is necessary? Am I to pile up arguments in favor of the excellence of prayer and its efficacy, drawing upon the experience of others, the renowned men of prayer? We are in a domain in which experience is individual or it is nothing. Am I to attempt to prove that prayer is good, still more, that my interlocutor, my reader, stands in need of it, when he doesn't even know it or feel it? If someone is not thirsty, how am I to prove to him that he is mistaken and that he is thirsty after all?—that he is in need after all of that water which I find to be so excellent? I shall never make him drink that way. At the very most, a physician treating a case of dehydration will order a perfusion for the patient whose sense of need is deadened and who does not want to drink—

but how is one to manage a perfusion of prayer? Something like that is what the Catholic Church had done with the communities of prayer. It does not seem to me to be well founded. So I shall not write an apology for prayer.

Finally, neither, shall I write a theology of prayer nor a biblical analysis on the subject of prayer. As we all know, there already are a thousand excellent theological books on the question. All has been said, all has been written on the subject. We already can know what there is to be known on the relation between the Holy Spirit and prayer, on the expression of faith, on the problem of answers to prayer, on the various types of prayer. What could I add to that? It would be mere repetition, and not as well said. And for the theology of prayer I can only refer the reader to Augustine or Theresa of Avila, to Luther or Pascal, to John of the Cross or to Barth, to Kierkegaard or to Calvin.* Furthermore, as has been pointed out (Maillot, *Vocabulaire biblique de Prière*): "To write a theology of prayer would be to write theology in its entirety." Such is not my intention.

What then? Then my aim will be much more modest. We are concerned with ourselves, with the actual situation of contemporary man, in our technical, technicalized society, with the situation of the person who does not want to pray because nothing invites him to do so, for whom everything is a deterrant from it. I shall not speak about the fact that man does not want to, or cannot, pray because he is a sinner. That has always been true. That is nothing new. But I ask myself, how does the situation look today? What is our society's mistake with regard to prayer? What are the obstacles to prayer? I cannot supply the remedies, but perhaps we shall be able to discover where we are, all of us, pious or not, believers or not. What are the motives which turn me

* See especially the splendid Chapter XX, Book III, of *The Institutes of the Christian Religion*.

aside from prayer? What possibilities do I have for undertaking it?

In other words, what, in this connection, are the features of sin today, in the reality of the present time? What is the current form, the contemporary expression, of man's alienation from God? I believe that we have entered, in fact, upon a human condition which is new. But given that condition, we must also state what the real facts *of* prayer are now, for with it all there are people who still pray. What are we to say? What then are we to do? What is the sense of this prayer? I shall go no further.

CONTENTS

1 : INTIMATE AND REASSURING VIEWS
OF PRAYER   3

> *Hands Bearing Gifts*   6
>
> *"Little Samuel"*   7
>
> *Heavenly Telephone*   8
>
> *Votive Plaques*   11
>
> *Millet's "Angelus"*   14
>
> *Dionysiac Prayer*   22
>
> *Self-Disciplinary Prayer*   25
>
> *Irresponsible Prayer*   27
>
> *The Prayer of Resignation*   30

ix

2 : THE FRAGILE FOUNDATIONS OF PRAYER   35

THE NATURAL FOUNDATION   35
The Argument   35
Objections to the Naturalistic Argument   39
A Comment on Function   41
An Untrustworthy Foundation   43

THE RELIGIOUS FOUNDATION   45
Pascal   45
Barth   47
The New Hermeneutic   50
The Inadequacy of Theology   52
PRAYER AS LANGUAGE   53
The Problems   54
The Essence of Prayer   61

3 : THE REASONS FOR NOT PRAYING   65

THE SOCIOLOGICAL REASONS   70
Secularization   71
The Climate of Reason and Skepticism   73
The Impracticality of Prayer   76
The Confusion of Prayer with Morality   80
The Breakdown of Language   82

THE THEOLOGICAL JUSTIFICATIONS   84
Man Come of Age   85
The Death of the Father   90

4 : THE ONLY REASON FOR PRAYING   99

    THE COMMANDMENT   102
    OBEDIENCE   110
    THE ASSERTION OF FREEDOM   120

5 : PRAYER AS COMBAT   139

    IN AN AGE OF ABANDONMENT   140
    Prayer and the Self   142
    The Achievement of Religionlessness   146
    The Only Weapon Against Falsehood   150

    AS COMBAT AGAINST GOD   153
    The Incognito of God   154
    A Combat of Total Involvement   160

    THE ACT OF HOPE   164
    The Ultimate Act   167
    Prayer and Social Participation   170
    Prayer and History   175

PRAYER AND MODERN MAN

1

INTIMATE AND REASSURING
VIEWS OF PRAYER

We are thinking of the celebrated sketch by Dürer of the joined hands of a man, in which fine precision is combined with profound expression—two working hands, strong, compact, muscular. This is not a person who is sick, or weak, or in need of prayer to compensate for his human deficiencies. This is a man in the complete sense of the word, a peasant or a warrior. Knotted veins run through those hands, as at a time of considerable exertion. For those hands prayer is not a commonplace, everyday act, carried out with routine indifference. They are the bearers of effort and concentration. The veins are swollen, as though the hands were on the hilt of a sword or on the handle of an ax. This is prayer seen as work, and as concentration of will.

Yet at the same time these hands are not clasped in passion, or fury, or tragedy. They are calm. There is no question of an exalted, or of a desperate, prayer. The word coming from the heart is not frenzied, is not grasping at straws. The hands are joined with great suppleness and delicacy. They scarcely press, the one against the other, at the tips of the fingers and at the palms. They are tranquil and at peace. They express the cessation of activity, the composure of heart which goes with a morning of promise or an evening of work completed.

But that simplicity does not bespeak ease. It conveys assurance. If the hands are joined so matter-of-factly, it is because the man knows to whom his prayer is addressed. He has no need of romantic or out-of-the-way gestures. In honest awareness he raises his hands in symbolic testimony to the unshakable power that dwells within his heart. He knows in whom he hopes. He knows in whom he believes. The linear purity of the gestures reminds us of the profound purity of faith. What we have here is a whole man in a whole faith.

The hands are joined like those of a vassal in the act of committing himself to the faithfulness of his lord. The gesture is identical. It conveys the same meaning. The vassal-to-be joined his hands together like those of Dürer's sketch, and he placed them, in all solemnity and responsibility, between the hands of his lord, who in turn joined his hands over those of his vassal. The latter then declared himself "the lord's man." It was a "commitment of trust." The man committed himself completely into the hands of his lord. He gave him his trust. And the lord completely accepted the vassal, assuming the responsibility before God and man. He, in his turn, gave the other his trust. But the lord, to be sure, was not accepting a vassal who was reduced, shoddy, deformed. He was dealing with a fighting man. The one who bowed low, who took on this posture of prayer, was a man whole and entire. The gesture of prayer was not a gesture of weakness.

This is recalled for us by the splendid passage from Charles Péguy's "The Mystery of the Holy Innocents":*

When Joinville falls on his knees on the stone floor
In the cathedral of Reims
Or in the chapel of his chateau at Joinville,
He is not an oriental slave
Who in fear, and in some craven and foul terror
Collapses before the knees and at the feet
Of an oriental potentate. He is a free man and a French baron,
Joinville, Lord of Joinville,
Who gives and who provides and who receives homage from
    others
Freely and, so to speak and in a certain sense without price
And a free man and a French baron.

Such is the first sublimity of the act of prayer which comes to light in the sketch by Dürer.

* The translation used here is by C. E. Hopkin.

Hands Bearing Gifts

But the action of the hands also calls to mind a very old proverb, "Empty hands, empty prayer," * which abruptly opens the door to the first in a series of misunderstandings, for these words do indeed characterize the prayer which is an act of complete self-giving. They say in the first instance that if I do not put my whole self into the prayer the latter is worthless. The gesture of the hands is there to witness to the fact that I renounce the use of power. My hands are joined, and so are no longer working or fighting. But they are a sort of cup in which I give back to the Lord all that I have done and all that I am. If they were only hands, if they were merely a sign signifying nothing, if they did not refer back to the whole person, if they were empty, then the prayer would make no sense.

But just at that point, beginning with those very words, we are led by perversity into other paths, and then we think: the hands should be full of offerings, of presents, of vows, of good deeds, so that God might pay attention to our prayer. If our hands should ever be empty of gifts and sacrifices, then we are sure that God would turn away. We often are tempted to explain in this way the lack of answers to our prayer. "I hadn't done enough . . . I lacked merit . . . I failed to make an offering"—strange conception of this God whom we think to entice like the gods of the pagans with our gifts, whom we expect to attract by our works! So

* Leroux de Linay, thirteenth century.

that when this God demands our all, our whole selves, because he has given his all, his whole self, when he asks our hearts and our love, when all of that can be indicated only by hands empty of things, yet full of faith and hope, by hands supplicating and adoring, stretched forth and joined; at that very point by a gross misunderstanding of his will we seek to fill our hands with things, which we bring in order to hide the fact that we are not bringing our lives and ourselves.

In prayer, God demands a free subject, who gives himself. We, for our part, would rather bring objects which we offer to him in order to make him amiable and understanding. Yet that is just when our hands are really empty because too full, and then we hear the loud voice saying to us again, "I hate, I despise your feasts, and I take no delight in your solemn assemblies" (Amos 5:21).

"Little Samuel"

Let us come down one step. Let us consider another picture of prayer, the little Samuel painted by Reynolds and reproduced on so many First Communion remembrance cards. He is a charming little fellow of four or five years of age, with a dimpled face and pretty curls neatly arranged, dressed in a lovely blouse. He is kneeling, and his eyes are raised in ecstasy to heaven. He folds his chubby little hands in a graceful gesture, while a heavenly light breaks through the darkness at the upper left of the canvas and falls upon the cherub. It is sweet, pleasing, comforting—all of which is supposed to be a rendition of the moving, gripping election of Samuel (I Samuel 3), that divine election which burst in at a time when "the word of the Lord was rare" and which fell upon a child who responded with the prayer, "Speak, for thy servant hears," and who began by receiving the tragic condemnation which he had to announce to Eli. The drama of the prayer is here reduced to the level of the pleasant, the consoling, the sweet, the banal, the ordinary. The prayer of little children is so nice. This is how the bourgeois mentality has appropriated the sublimity of prayer to its own ends and has sugar-coated it. That picture, so widely distributed, is only a first lie concerning prayer. We shall come upon many others and we must become acquainted with them in order to know where we are, how we are to picture for ourselves this decisive moment in the encounter with God.

Heavenly Telephone

Here, starting from a good intention, is a formula borrowed from a Salvation Army hymn, that of "the heavenly telephone." Is not prayer a direct communication with God? Is it not the assured means of telling him what we have to say, and of hearing his word in our hearts? There is constant talk of changing the traditional terminology of Christianity in order to find models adapted to modern man. What is the result? Prayer has become the heavenly telephone, and all good people will immediately understand. After all, there is "the hot line" to Moscow. Why should there not be a device for communicating with someone who is about as far away as the Kremlin? The obvious parallel brings the event within the complete understanding of everyone, the more so since it has to do with a kind of instrument, in short a gadget. I hold my prayer as a person would who is listening on a telephone, and I talk into it. Predictably it works. The similarity assures me that the prayer is heard, just as I can be certain that, thanks to the telephone, my correspondent hears me no matter how far apart we are. Thus the device itself gives me assurance because a means is at hand and I can do something.

And this, perfectly adapted as it is to the mentality of modern man, reveals a frightful misunderstanding. With such a model as our point of departure, how are we to grasp the fact that prayer precisely is not a means of laying hold of God; that prayer precisely is not made possible by a system, but, rather, by a free decision of grace on the part of the one who wills indeed to listen; that prayer precisely is not addressed to one who *dwells at a distance,* but is addressed to one who *comes very close* (even into our hearts!); that prayer precisely is a miracle and not a technical procedure. Truly we are beset on all sides by misunderstandings!

Confusedly, but movingly, the experience of the great mystics still attracts us. Prayer becomes a second state. Whether suddenly or gradually, the person ceases to be conscious of self. He is no longer capable of speaking. He no longer designates the petitions and the moment of encounter with God. He even passes beyond speaking with tongues (glossolalia), in order to live in a state in which his blurred senses no longer relate to the particular but bring him into a knowledge of inexpressible awarenesses, presences, truths.

What the youth of today seek in drugs the mystics have always found in prayer. They describe it as an encounter with God, but it is just as much a fusion with the great All. It is the way of the dark night of the soul of John of the Cross, or of the ineffable presence disclosed to Teresa of Avila. There is no more vision, no more knowledge. It is the inexpressible, the prayer beyond all prayer. The latter then appears as a stage in the development of the experience. But in the meeting with God, or in the fusion, there no longer is any prayer properly so called, since nothing in the realm of knowledge or cogency can any longer be said.

This tendency is very foreign to the Protestant mentality, which is always more or less rational. Yet we need to ask ourselves whether it is not just as valid as the shoddy discourse too often called prayer. The mystic experience frightens us. We feel embarrassed to recognize it. We distrust it. And yet, if prayer is indeed a speaking with God face to face, how could we remain the forlorn inmates of the commonplace? Why does not this presence of God work a transformation within us? We are not changed by our own prayer for the reason that we think about God with far too great familiarity. We are vulgarly, tritely accustomed to him. We treat him casually. Speaking to him does not strike us as a unique and stupefying experience. I am not saying, of course, that the mystical experience is the test of a truly profound prayer, but, rather, that our prayer, which assuredly never takes us that far, is the test of an absence of prayer!

Furthermore, though we distrust mysticism, we nevertheless have retained its formulas in many of our liturgies, specifically in connection with prayer. Do we not say, "Let us lift up our hearts (or our minds) in prayer"?—an old expression. St. John of Damascus, as early as the eighth century, said that prayer was "an elevation of the mind to God." We have very generally retained this imagery without the slightest conception of what it really means; what implications, what consequences it could have if it were actually so—if in place of a simple attitude of recollection there were a veritable elevation to God!

But it is no more than a formula, the content of which, moreover, seems to us to be suspect. We know from Bishop Robinson that God is not "up there," so what could "lift up" mean? We know from the sociology of behavior that the mind is not an entity separable from the body. Finally, we know from the Reformers that man can never under any circumstances "lift himself up to God." That does not depend upon man's will, but on the will of God. So this allows us easily to dispose of the mystical experience of prayer. *Perhaps* in that case we are missing a profound truth.

Votive Plaques

There is a strange custom in France which consists of inscribing prayers on the votive plaques erected in churches. These graffiti, occasionally in large numbers, according to the importance of the saint or of the veneration accorded the statue of the Virgin of that region, are surely a most direct expression of popular prayer. They are often very moving, sometimes funny or astonishing. There are requests by the thousands for success in school examinations, requests to be loved by "X," or to be healed. Those are the three most fre-

quent themes, but there are some which are quite personal
and unusual. "Arrange it so that he is the first to get mad,"
asks one woman who wants a divorce but does not want to
be the one to take the initiative. "Let me find work before
tomorrow so that I can feed my little daughter." "Give me
the courage to jump by parachute." These inscriptions reveal the true content of popular prayer, always quite simple, very concrete, very immediate. Not once have I seen a
request for the Holy Spirit. We can only be persuaded that
such is indeed the content of the prayers of millions of Christians.

But the fact of their being inscribed is itself noteworthy.
It is as though the word alone were not sufficient. Writing
is more substantial, more durable, engages more the person
who does it. To go so far as to write the prayer endows it
with a more intense fervor. Moreover, *Verba volant, scripta
manent.* After all, words fly away just as much for the saint
or for the Virgin. What is needed is a more lasting evidence,
a sort of permanent prayer which remains before the eyes
of the saint. He ceases to hear the word which I said only
once (so convinced are we finally of the anthropomorphism
of God and of his entourage), but here I have written it in
front of him, and he will read it and reread it, even after I
am no longer there, even when I no longer am thinking
about it.

Also, to write it on a votive plaque links it in some way
with the answer to the preceding prayer. Since the person
who gave this votive offering had his prayer answered, his
prayer must indeed have been potent. I am, in a sense,
putting mine under the benefit of his. What is more, I am

placing it under the benefit of his thanksgiving expressed in the votive plaque. Hence I expect the saint to be favorably disposed. Since "X," for his part, has offered this testimony of his gratitude, the saint who sees it should be pleased with it, and if I write my prayer on this votive plaque he will easily accept it together with the gift which is being made to him.

Such are the explanatory features of this custom. We are in out-and-out paganism, you say? Assuredly the urge for the permanence of a prayer which has to be repeated indefinitely is a throwback toward the style of the prayer wheel, this word strangely detached from the person who says it, yet which is credited with having been spoken by him each time the little piece of paper containing the prayer reaches a certain position, whenever the written prayer is henceforth made permanent. I need no longer occupy myself with it. The prayer which once was word and personal involvement has acquired a sort of special life of its own and keeps on going without my having to be involved with it any further.

Magic perhaps; but in that case one would have to make the distinction of that which is not magic in the prayer of the pious and genuine Christian. It is not so simple. To expect an answer to prayer, to claim to influence the will of God, is not that already magic of sorts? The prayer which we want to be so upright and unalloyed, moving between the domain of mysticism and that of magic, seems to me to be treading a very narrow path. But there are other limits as well.

Millet's "Angelus"

Let us consider Millet's "Angelus." Two peasants have stopped in the evening after a day of work in the fields, the hoe allowed to drop suddenly, the bag of potatoes only half filled. They have stopped because a bell is ringing to summon them, three strokes, in the Name of the Father and of the Son and of the Holy Spirit. Then the changes peal forth for the beginning of the prayer. They have stopped at the end of their day of work. The sunset sheds its light upon them. They are in their soiled clothes and their hands are caked with earth. They are still sweating from their hard labor. It is those hands which they join. It is in those clothes that they respond to the summons of the bell. They are absorbed in earnest prayer.

Perhaps the famous painting is bad. Its meaning fully reconstitutes what the Church had in mind in establishing the angelus as a prayer for morning, midday, and evening, at the place of work and in the clothing of work, hence closely intertwined with commonplace existence. Still, as a prayer it is quite other than that simple earthiness. It introduces the spiritual dimension into everyday activity, and hence is an element of rupture. It forces man to look from a different angle upon the work from which he has just detached himself. The angelus is at one and the same time the moment of detachment and yet the bond, the connection, with everything to which we are attached.

In its full significance this ancient Catholic custom is very beautiful, but for us it raises two questions concerning prayer, which moreover are quite diverse. The first has to do with the dreadful motto, "To work is to pray," dreadful because of the cynicism, the justification, the contempt which it expresses. Oh, I know all the possible theological justifications! Work is willed by God. Work fulfills man's destiny. Work serves to complete nature, which is only in the rough. Work turns nature to the glory of God. When all that is put together, we see clearly that there no longer is any need to pray, for given those conditions work is itself a prayer.

Very well, I declare that all that is a lie, because if we took seriously the "theological" affirmations concerning work we would at the same time be obliged to remember the commandment to keep holy the day of rest, and to recollect the specific character of prayer in relation to activity. I call these "theological" explanations lies because they are nothing more or less than justifications for continuing to work without pause, without turning toward God, without praying at the hour of the angelus. Precisely if I say that work is the carrying out of a vocation to which God has called me, I cannot at the same time say that "to work is to pray."

The motto in question is an invention of the bourgeoisie for affirming the sanctity of work, for justifying oneself before men (how could it be before God?), for proclaiming the sanctity of one's "religion of work," and of the implacable discipline of work which it imposes on others. The worker has no need of free time for prayer. In the factory there need be no stopping, no pause. When the factory lets out at the end of the day, what does it matter that the worker is staggering with fatigue, unable to put two ideas together, that he is filled with rebellious hatred for his exploiter, and hence is incapable of the peace which is necessary for prayer. What does it matter? Thanks to the employer this profane worker has prayed whether he wanted to or not, ten or twelve hours a day. Such is the frightful lie which the bourgeoisie, the management, have proclaimed for a hundred and fifty years to maintain a religious façade and to assure a strict totalitarian regime of work.

The Catholic Church in her wisdom knew that to work is precisely not to pray, and that it was necessary to interrupt work in order to stand for a while before the Lord, to offer up the work done or to be done, to sanctify those works, to be with God other than in the performance of hard labor. "Other than," and yet not other than, because the one who prays is still fully involved in the daily round. His work shoes are imbedded in that soil. It is not necessary to be in Sunday clothes in order to pray, but it is necessary to interrupt one's work. We are not, to be sure, to separate ourselves from our work, yet prayer detaches us from work. It frees us from it. It puts work exactly in its lowly but necessary place. Such is the first aspect of prayer, so just and profound, which is evoked by the angelus.

The second is important but difficult to explain fully. The angelus? A prayer on command. A bell rings. Immediately everything stops. One has been thinking about almost anything, when all of a sudden he is supposed to think about God. One is not in the "required disposition"? What difference does that make? At a given moment one must pray, an obligatory prayer, an automated prayer (For it must not be forgotten that the prayer recited at that moment is not spontaneous. It is the recitation of words learned by heart. But where is the heart?), and it is clear right away what the various dimensions are: liturgical prayer, prayer presumed to take place under certain circumstances, the discipline of prayer.

The theological basis for this is obvious enough. God is always present, always available. At whatever moment in which one turns to him the prayer is received, is heard, is authenticated, for it is God who gives our prayer its value and its character, not our interior dispositions, not our fervor, not our lucidity. The prayer which is pronounced for God and accepted by him becomes, by that very fact, a true prayer. That is the first point.

Also, at whatever moment in which man might be summoned to pray, if the prayer is sufficiently important to him, if he has comprehended the extraordinary gravity of this act, if he is imbued with the importance of his being present before God, then that conviction is incommensurate with his attachments, distractions, and occupations. The awesomeness, the seriousness of prayer surpasses, dominates all the rest, and this rest should be blotted out the moment the prayer begins. If that were not the case it would be because he is not convinced of the importance of the prayer. Then it would depend indifferently on his needs and dispositions, which reduces it to very little indeed. That is the second point.

With regard to the third point, it assuredly has to do with the community of believers, the Church. Prayer must be an action of the community, because God wills us to be bound to one another by a tie of love. Prayer is never empty and superficial when it is liturgical, because then it is said by the

choirs of angels together with the Church. It is never mechanical when it is ordered by the Church, because it is taken
up by the brethren, each in support of the other, the faith of
the one making up the deficiency of the other. Barth has
written unforgettable pages on the importance of liturgical
and community prayer.

Yet it is difficult not to recall those "vain repetitions"
which Jesus rejects. It is difficult not to wonder about it,
when you see that it is just that which led the Catholic
Church to institute the litanies, the rosaries, the prayers repeated automatically a hundred times, the same words but
without meaning in the final analysis. Can one go all the way
in saying that it is God who validates our prayer, so why
worry about paying attention? Surely not! But how could I
put myself wholly into a prayer when the latter is on command, at a specified hour, and is composed of fixed formulas?

We need, to be sure, to be distrustful of "Protestant indi-
vidualism" and of the "dispositions" for prayer. I can feel
completely disposed to pray, but what content am I going
to give to this spontaneous prayer? The graffiti that we
mentioned above reveal indeed the content of individual
prayers, and the result is not particularly satisfying! They
are not superior for being spontaneous. In this case it is the
theme of the prayer (too often focused on the self, its interests and preoccupations) which is of poor, sometimes
shameful quality.

However, with prayer that is liturgical, or on command,
it is the earnestness of the prayer which is in question. Everyone knows how difficult it is to join fully in prayer said
by an officiant, and there are no devices or procedures for

earnestly doing so. The moment one introduces artificial means into prayer, the latter ceases to be prayer. Perhaps it is a weakening of faith, a staleness, which makes it hard to-day to participate in collective prayer on command. Perhaps it is the added demand and the added seriousness which makes us face up to what we are doing whenever we take on the appearance of prayer without the reality.

In the same category of ideas, we find ourselves very critical in the presence of the obligatory prayer at the opening of the business meetings of the Church, such as presbyteral and regional councils. Persons charged with a ministry, those who manage the finances, or are responsible for the Church's strategy, or exercise authority, feel obligated to pray whenever they meet together. The intention certainly is good, that of placing whatever one is about to do in this domain "before the eyes of God." Surely these persons in responsible positions should be able to pray together. Why, then, does it seem so formal, so external, so meaningless? I no longer can stand the endless invocations of the Holy Spirit. I no longer can believe in any action pertaining to this category of prayer.

At a time when we are so manifestly deprived of the presence and power of the Holy Spirit, what meaning do those prayers of petition have? We know in advance that if ever they were answered, if ever the Holy Spirit were given, it would overturn all the financial plans, all the projections for the future, all the wise administrations. Even when the person saying them is filled with piety, they are purely formal prayers to cover the mediocrity of our decisions. They are a kind of official prayer, which allows us afterward to manage according to our own ideas, with our weaknesses and incapacities, an affair which we acknowledge belongs to God, yet without giving him the slightest chance to express his will. They are prayers which serve to give us a good conscience while resigning ourselves to the fact that the Church is still the mediocre affair we know it to be. They are fictitious prayers, which say with the lips that we are in the service of the Lord, when in fact we are carrying on our business quite by ourselves. They are covering prayers, putting us right with God at the opening of the session; then, since we have called upon him, we feel all the more free not to take the Lord into account during the course of the discussions. I have always felt that these prayers fell upon a great silence, and that the only reply we received was from the void. I have always been humiliated whenever I was called upon to offer up such prayers at such meetings, acceding by social convention to an action which I clearly saw was an affront to the honor of God.

By contrast, in the category of obligatory prayers, those which answer to personal discipline seem to me to be more earnest, although always difficult, and sometimes suspect. The prayer before meals is, to be sure, excellent for dedicating those good things to God, and for thanking him for giving them to us. But here again, how often are these prayers a simple formality, gotten over with fast, an irksome duty which must be gone through with before "diving in"!

Prayer at a fixed hour—we know that some people undertake the discipline of praying in the midst of their work whenever the clock strikes the hour. A few moments of meditation break into the frantic course of activity at each hour of the day. That is good, but it must not be forgotten that insofar as it is a matter of another device to oblige one to pray by outward discipline it can very quickly become nothing more than an automation, producing a prayer without real content. Nevertheless, this rule has the great merit of a break inserted into the actual course of life. It is an individual and voluntary substitute for the angelus.

We conclude this summary of prayer "on order," or arising out of social obligation, by citing one of the most explosive formulas ever encountered, taken from a letter from Madame de Maintenon to M. d'Aubigné, and referring to her daughter: "May she pray in public every day. Remember that one owes this example to one's domestic servants." Thus prayer becomes a public formality with a purely sociological purpose. Religion is good for the common people. We others, of course, we intellectuals, even if we believe in God, have no need of pretenses like prayer, worship, etc. But those slightly ridiculous things are necessary if the domestics are to be obedient and devoted. Prayer as a means of social conformity, as an insurance for the ruling class, as a strengthening of its authority, what a marvelous hypocrisy that is, what a clear-cut disobedience to Jesus Christ, who commanded us not to pray before men and not to make a public display of piety.

It is true that the situation in France today is somewhat changed by comparison with the seventeenth century To pray in public outside a church today is, rather, to invite ridicule and to become the butt of jokes. Yet one must never forget that one is a Christian and subject to the tendency to use the highest appointments of the faith by turning them away from their true significance and calling. That is why the command of Jesus is still applicable, because of the ever-present threat of perverting prayer.

Dionysiac Prayer

The style of prayer at the opposite pole from disciplined prayer is the Dionysiac, frenetic prayer, the exalted prayer of small, fervent groups whose pietism is sincere but dubious. This is prayer thought of as a prayer of abundance, in which the person sets forth everything that is going through his head. But again, if it really were a matter of everything that was going through one's head, it could be accepted. Why not tell God everything that wells up from the bottom of the heart? Alas, those verbose, diffuse, overflowing, interminable prayers are not honest precisely inasmuch as they are the indefinite spinning out of ready-made formulas, the mass production of all the clichés that have been learned for generations.

I certainly do not call in question the sincerity and the piety of those who give themselves over to this practice, but I note that there is nothing authentic in the expression of this faith. The deluge of words in a monotone, the outburst of commonplaces, of exclamations, of interjections, the pseudo-glossolalia which are nothing but a banality, in reality all that is a cover for an absence of the spirit of prayer. We know all too well those interminable discourses addressed to God, which some find a deadly bore, while others, for the most part, warm progressively to the rhythm, the bodily posture remaining motionless for a long time until the accompanying psychological fixation induces a certain blurring of the mind.

Can prayer consist of this accumulation of words, when Jesus has commanded us precisely to avoid vain repetitions? Can prayer be a means of carrying the faithful to a certain pitch of excitement, with the purpose of destroying critical awareness in favor of an uncontrolled effusion? Should prayer be a sort of mystic practice, running away from reason in order to turn into exaltation, to the point of convulsions of the body, meaningless exclamations, frothing at the mouth, and rolling of the eyes?

Once again, the true presence of the Lord can make a powerful impact on a man. Really to be one who is speaking to God can be profoundly disturbing. My body can in fact tremble if God is the friend to whom I am speaking. This presence can be so powerful that I can lose control of my words and movements. But it is blasphemous to arrive at the psychological result by imitating that which can (after the fact) attest to the relationship with the Lord, to arrive at it by methods designed to produce an illusion that the Lord is present. In that case it is plainly demonic. Of course a person can imitate the work of God, can easily reproduce by artifice that which (sometimes) takes place at the approach of the Lord. But this frothing, these convulsions, these exclamations, this delirium, are then the reverse of true prayer. On the one hand, they are induced in order to make people believe that God is present, and yet, on the other hand, they are a sort of magic procedure for forcing the God to come.

I say "the God" because this Dionysiac prayer is found in all religions, and the Pythian priestess revealed the divine pronouncements with frothing at the mouth and convulsions. So there is nothing specifically Christian in this exalted, diffuse, intense prayer. The intensity is not a sign of the truth of Jesus Christ. It can be very nice to have experiences of that kind, but one must remember that the experiences are evidence only of a certain phenomenological continuity among religions. They are a reminder that *at that time* the revelation of God *also* gave rise to a religion.

We must, of course, extend these observations to danced prayers. One occasionally admires such a vigorous expression of lofty tension, but is it spiritual? Yes, if in the use of that word we are not thinking of the Holy Spirit, but simply of the spirit of man. Leaps and shakings, invocations repeated a hundred times over in a shrill voice, the clapping of the hands, beating time with the entire body until suddenly one of the participants who is laid hold of by God begins the dance of the possessed—for some that is the highest expression of prayer. Here again, we are obliged to point out that this is the same phenomenon as that which characterized the whirling dervishes, shamanism, etc., and that to attach the name of Jesus Christ to it is simply demonic. There is no expression there of the nearness of the Lord. It is useless to cite David's dance before the Ark as a justification of these dances. I do not find the citation of a biblical text convincing in view of the survival of such psychic phenomena in all religious forms.

If one would conform to a true prayer before God, one

would need firmly to reject these seductive temptations which carry a sort of label of authenticity. Unfortunately it is the label of a false authenticity, one which man authenticates for himself when he confuses his own psychic phenomena with the hidden but solemn presence of the Lord of his life. When faced with each Dionysiac expression of prayer we must return doggedly to the strict affirmation that the spirit of Dionysius is the reverse of the Spirit of the Lord.

Self-Disciplinary Prayer

"We do not offer up prayers to God in order to instruct him, but to put ourselves in the good dispositions in which we should be toward him." In this thought, Bossuet gives us a picture of prayer which is current among pious and wise people. What sound thinking, apparently! It is certainly true, is it not, that God who knows everything is not dependent upon our prayers for his knowledge of our needs, nor even for his knowledge of our attitudes toward him. Must we conclude, then, that prayer is useless? We shall encounter this problem again later. Such a conclusion results from a false conception of the relationship established by God between man and himself.

At this point we limit ourselves to the consideration of a view of prayer which is more widespread than one would think, namely, that the content of prayer is not so important in the final analysis (and of course this is supported also by the passage from Paul witnessing to the fact that we never truly know what we should ask for in our prayers). What counts in prayer is the posture, the getting down on one's knees, the joining of the hands, the bowed head, the presentation of the self before God, "to put ourselves in the good dispositions in which we should be. . . ." Prayer in this view is a means of acting upon ourselves pedagogically, and of making ourselves be what God expects us to be.

Again, with a different nuance, a different orientation, we are discovering the same desire to make prayer into a means, an instrument, a method, that is to say, to divert it radically from that which God himself has appointed it to be. It is another simple and reassuring view of prayer. Of the extraordinary, outrageous, astonishing act, we retain the system brought down to our own level. It is obviously true, is it not, that we make no claim to acting upon God to modify his will or to change his purpose. We are too modest for that. Our prayer, in the end, is only meant to be an action upon ourselves. It is self-instruction.

With what seeming wisdom and humility do we in fact divert prayer hypocritically from its truth in which God is at the center, in order to put ourselves once again at the center of the operation. Thus to pretend that God is too great is a subtle way of recovering the principal role for ourselves. It is a way of not obeying the order established by God, and of recovering for our own account that which escapes us, since it is God who has given it. Here we must learn anew that prayer is not what we, in our intelligence and good will, would like it to be, but that it can only be the expression of our obedience when we accept it for what God reveals to us that it is. In the realm of prayer we can make no other claim than to obey.

Irresponsible Prayer

"Disincarnate prayers, self-satisfaction with our good feelings, prayer for others which permits us not to do anything for them, such prayers are a substitute for action, a cheap way of having a good conscience. They are a lie and a hypocrisy whenever we have given up our own effectiveness, our own means, in order to place all in the hands of God. Having done that, we feel justified in not getting involved, in not giving evidence of any effective action, in not concerning ourselves with the welfare of others." This contention has been put forward hundreds of times in recent years. It is, to be sure, partly true. Surely it can seem too easy to pray at the bedside of a sick person, then to depart, leaving him alone with his sickness; to pray for a family in distress without adding to the prayer the money to resolve its problems; to pray for the peoples of the world who are suffering from famine, oppression, or exploitation, without taking part in the political struggle against social injustice.

In the face of this position on disincarnate prayer the watchword has become: "Prayer requires that we do ourselves that which we ask God to do." If I ask for *us* (and not for *me!*) *our* daily bread, I shall myself give this bread to those around me who lack it. If I pray for peace, I should undertake concretely to establish peace. This new attitude carries much weight. It teaches us quite rightly that prayer does not consist of words in thin air, and that a person cannot pray unless he is fully responsible for what he is saying. He must be completely involved in the action. It is an interpretation which can be supported by biblical examples and theological arguments. When Jesus Christ is about to work the multiplication of the loaves, he says to his disciples, "*You* give them something to eat." What is more, he takes the five loaves and the seven fish belonging to a child, and he uses these as the base, the raw material for the miracle.

So we say, "I pray that God may act, but his action will be in and through that which I am prepared to do [it will not be from the sky above], and it will be in and through what I myself give that the miracle will take place [it will not be *ex nihilo*]. I am not capable of much. I cannot myself heal the sick person, nor feed that hungry person, but if I do what I can in my own sphere then God works the miracle, which consists precisely in the fact that out of such inadequate means great things are brought to pass." That is true, and beyond dispute biblically, provided always that we do not then slip into that little variation so frequently met with today: ". . . then God performs the miracle *which consists* precisely in the fact that I who am bad, egotistical, sinful, that I have become capable of this love, this charity." Indeed not! The miracle is not that the disciples should be involved in the action, but that the five thousand people were fed.

That variation brings us again face to face with our unbelief, our lack of daring, and back again, finally, to the gravity of prayer. It shows up our lack of earnestness in shutting ourselves up in the exclusive circle of the humanly possible. It allows us to eliminate the miracle and to dispense with God's decision.

But let us return to the true interpretation. It states the profound theological truth, namely, that God appoints us as collaborators, and wills not to act except through human mediation. In this sense, of course, it is seen to be well founded. Alas, that does not exhaust its meaning, for the deep-seated tendency now is really to place man at the center of everything. In insisting that man must himself perform that which he petitions, we no longer are saying that he should become involved in it, but that he is in fact responsible for fulfilling the prayer himself. The answer no longer depends upon someone outside who acts *proprio motu,* but upon what I myself shall do. This activity takes precedence over the prayer itself, which has now become the program for my own action.

This interpretation corresponds exactly to the society in which we find ourselves, namely, a world of means. The means (techniques) proliferate. We are equipped with countless appliances, media, methods, instruments, organizations. With this view of prayer the ends tend everywhere to thin out. The means increase. The means are at hand, at my disposal. This teaching is saying to us, "Use to the full the means which this society gives you, then you will see." In other words, the proliferation of means alters the character of prayer. It is no longer a giving over of what I can do into the hands of God, upon whom I call for help from the depths of my impotence, "Out of the depths I cry to thee, O Lord!" Today there are thousands of ways to fill up the depths, or in fact to avoid them. Why call upon God?

It is indeed true, of course, that prayer should not be a resignation. It is indeed true that it should come into play only after man has carried out all that is possible, that it should not be for the lack of what man could have done:

"I have fought well, and God alone can give the victory."
Yet prayer in the Scriptures is also a renunciation of human
means. It is not merely the point beyond which I could not
go, the limit of my power which dissolves into impotence,
but it is indeed a stripping bare, the abandonment of all
human apparatus in order to place myself, without arms
or equipment, into the hands of the Lord, who decides and
fulfills. There is in this a narrow path between laziness
and power, between bustle which blots out all relationship
with God (Martha and Mary) and cowardly resignation. It
is a narrow path in which prayer has two faces: one *a saying
to God that I have done everything within my power,* the
other, *a complete surrender of the decision to God, in which
I no longer offer as proof of my sincerity an action which I
have carried out to the end, but a renunciation of the possibilities of my own strength and initiative.* Each of these two
faces contains as much truth as the other. Neither can be
effaced. The vision of prayer here under review eliminates
the second of the two, and thereby transforms the first. In
the degree in which the truth of renouncing my own powers disappears, prayer itself changes. It is no longer addressed to the Lord, but to myself.

The Prayer of Resignation

That brings us to the most profound hypocrisy of man in
this domain. As was to be expected, it has to do with the
most profound truth: "Thy will be done," "Not my will,
but thine," "Always, Lord, not what I will, but what thou

wilt." What more can you say in prayer? You would seem to have voiced the most exalted, the most profound, the truest of all prayer. Does not all piety spring finally from this renunciation? Is not the central point of all prayer that in which I recognize the absolute independence, the sovereignty, the authority of the Lord, wherein I give myself up filially to his will which can only be good, wherein I witness to the genuineness of my faith?

And yet, that profound prayer is not true or sincere of itself. How often have we heard it, and pronounced it ourselves, as a statement of sloth, and I go so far as to say as a statement of an absence of faith. That prayer is a prayer of resignation. I have no genuine will. I am not a man who is standing upright, struggling, working. I am giving myself up. All possible ambiguities are present in the self-abandonment of a little child in the arms of his father. There is the giving up of pride and excess, which is good, but there is also inertia, impotence (not that which I recognize after having gone to the limit of my powers, but the impotence of the shoddy, the incapable, the stupid), and there is cowardice. There is the too-frequent attitude of Christians for whom faith is one more convenience, and this prayer is a convenience of faith. Thus the high point of trust may be no more than the high point of futility. What is more, it can mean, "What is the point of tiring myself out? God in any event will only do what he has in mind, and in the final analysis whatever happens will always be God's will."

The twofold sin of this beautiful prayer is then plainly evident. On the one hand, there is a sort of basic mistrust of God. He is the despot who will never do anything except his own will. Of course, I can appeal to him, but I know that whatever I might say is of no avail, and I take shelter finally behind this last formula, which implies my fundamental unbelief in the God who is good, Father, Love. I address myself to the tyrant, and I say to him, "May thy will be done, since I know very well that thou wilt never do anything other than thy will, and that nothing is left for me to do but to give in."

Prayer then becomes a means of hiding, of avoiding the questions of God and of real life. We speak in order not to say what we are doing. We (falsely) leave everything to God in order not to be accountable for what we are doing. We pray thus in order not to say what we are, in order to put on a disguise, and to have nothing more in common with that God, for this prayer can *also* be the rejection of truth.

But from another angle there is a still more serious factor. I am prepared to recognize all events as the expression of the will of God. Ultimately, anything whatsoever becomes the will of God. It is then the prayer of the absence of faith, because it is the prayer of indifference, based on the conviction of the impossibility of communicating with God or of cooperating with him. It is a formula thrown in on the off chance, a prayer out of the fear of passing something up!

Hence we should not put our confidence in a formula, even in one derived from Scripture, however pious it may appear to be. Its content can vary greatly. It can be sin. Satan can express himself in it. Prayer is not an act which goes without saying. It can never enclose itself in formulas. It implies a certain lucidity, a certain resolution.

What have we done in running through these most usual and customary, these "intimate and reassuring" views of prayer? We have simply tried to establish where we are, not the theologians or, on the other hand, the unbelievers, but the simple faithful of all the churches. What does it mean to them, to us, to pray? What are we really doing? What do we have in mind when we come to pray? For that has to be our point of departure if we are to know what prayer really is in our society. The purest and the most sublime spiritual flights, the most profound and learned theological definitions, are powerless before the fact that modern man is praying less and less, and that even for the most earnest Christians there is a certain hesitation, a certain difficulty in praying.

These flash views make no pretense of telling us what prayer is, but, rather, how modern man lives prayer. They present an inconsistent, sometimes conflicting landscape, yet those chaotic aspects are in themselves extraordinarily illuminating.

2 ✣

THE FRAGILE FOUNDATIONS
OF PRAYER

In the attempt to certify the validity, the soundness, and the enduring character of prayer, two foundations for this human act have always been recognized. In brief let us say that they are human nature and the presence of God, a natural foundation and a theological foundation. We need to ask ourselves whether or not these are still valid today, and that will lead us to investigate prayer as language.

THE NATURAL FOUNDATION

The Argument

All men in their desires and fears invoke the aid of a divinity. Some philosophers more respectful toward the Supreme Being and less condescending to human weakness would have reduced all prayer to resignation. We know no religion without prayer. Thus, in substance, did Voltaire affirm the historical permanence of this fact. Obviously one can and did pass quickly enough from the observation of historical permanence to an affirmation about basic human nature: it is man's nature to appeal to a Supreme Being, an Almighty. Man has never been able to live without praying. It is one of the very dimensions of his being. Each time man begins to awake to the consciousness of self he has prayed, perhaps even before, if it be admitted that the prehistoric drawings and sculptures are symbolic representations of prayer. That which has been universal and lasting should not be treated as contingent and accidental. If the occurrence is, without fail, repeated, that means that it is more than itself. It indicates that behind the repetition there is a constraining reality. Man finds as a given thing within himself the imperative of prayer.

But also, prayer is the highest communication. It is not merely a mystical outpouring, but in the degree in which man is a being in communication and cannot be otherwise, there has to be an archetype of this communication which is prayer. Thus it is not only the historical permanence of prayer but also the ontological reality of it which leads us to recognize a natural reality in prayer, and a spontaneity as well.

Is it because parents teach prayers to their children that the latter are turned all their lives toward a beyond which seems to them to cast a halo over everything? Or are we indeed in the presence of that reality which the romantics saw so well? Is it not true after all, apart from all acculturation, that a great spectacle of nature moves us and incites us to speak to an Unknown, not to self or to neighbor, but to him whom these wonderful things seem to denote? In a state of exaltation aroused by the ocean, a mountain, a storm, the lunar splendor, the crimson sunset, every man sings the glory of the Creator. It is the prayer to the Supreme Being, the All, the Invisible, prayer which will take different forms according to cultural differences but the spontaneity of which appears nevertheless to be located beyond the learning process. Such is the confession of the *Vicaire Savoyard,* and no doubt Rousseau was not mistaken. Victor Hugo, for his part, makes prayer more than a spontaneous act of man. The whole of nature is itself a prayer to God:

> And the birds, turned toward him whom all things name,
> Something of man to God perhaps proclaim
> While singing their sacred hymn.*

Prayer appears to spring to the lips directly from the heart. It seems to be something more profound, more simple, more direct, more spontaneous in the reality of man, for he is speaking to the Unknown as to the commander in chief of his powers and at the same time as to the one who can hear and understand. That was not invented. Man has always lived it and recognized it.

So runs the initial statement of the theme. Yet today, as a matter of fact, we seem to be faced with another reality. The man of these times does not seem so responsive to those effusions. Nature disappears and no longer inspires him. It

* This translation is by C. E. Hopkin.

disappears because technology effaces it and corrupts it materially, because science desacralizes it. Can I still be moved by the divine Ishtar when I know that human footsteps are imprinted in the dust of her countenance? Nor does the social world in which we are favor prayer. On the contrary, it seems to deny it, to divert man from it.

Just the same, for those who look upon prayer as an expression of man's nature, there remains the strong argument of the new religions. It is precisely the modern political movements which are restoring to prayer its current relevance. What was the exalted ecstasy of the young Nazis toward Hitler if it wasn't prayer? And we know how many of these young men died fervently pronouncing the name of Hitler, just as the Christian martyrs pronounced the name of Jesus Christ. Hitler was right when he said that he heard the soul of his people rising toward him in a gigantic prayer. There was exactly the same phenomenon with Stalin. The devotional discourse, the incantation, which recurred endlessly on the airwaves of the Soviet radio was a prayer. The constant repetition of the name Joseph Vissarionovich Stalin in these discourses and acclamations of the crowd was a litany, and we were faced with innumerable texts of veritable prayers addressed to this Almighty, asking efficiency at work and prosperity for Communism.

Today we are witnessing the identical phenomenon with Mao. He has succeeded in working a truly remarkable miracle. He has succeeded in giving religion to the Chinese people, who by historical tradition and moral training could be characterized as the least religious people on earth. Prayer has now become a permanent practice. Such is the fervent glorification of the Name. Such is the waving of the little red book, an amulet identical with all the fetishes of the past. There are even prayers with verbal content. One prays to Mao to make it stop raining, to protect from illness, hence quite classical prayers.

Let us say, then, that what is tending to disappear is prayer to an invisible God, having a spiritual quality, and most particularly prayer of the Christian type. But there is being substituted prayer which is political in origin, addressed to a divinized man exercising omnipotence. Prayer has changed its character and its object, yet the phenomenon of prayer persists, which tends to demonstrate its validity as something given in nature.

Objections to the Naturalistic Argument

There is much to object to in the whole argument based on nature, even if one acknowledges the accuracy of the political mutation of prayer. In the first place let us remember that the ethnologists would certainly not be in agreement on the universality of the phenomenon. A number of so-called primitive societies have not known, and do not know, prayer. Acts and words which are not prayer had often wrongly been interpreted as prayer when seen through Western concepts and customs. Prayer is absent from the relations with nature and with the group as Lévy-Strauss describes them. Hence, one cannot depend upon historical permanence in order to be assured of its natural character and of its ability to endure through the current crisis. Intellectually there is no basis for saying that modern man's abandonment of prayer is a mere accident, and that the nature which inclines man to pray will regain the upper hand, especially since one would have to be quite clear about what it is that gives rise to this prayer. Is it the expression of an inherent nature, or is it in consequence of a certain situation? Voltaire's thought, cited above, alludes to this: "All men in their desires and fears. . . ." Prayer takes place when man desires something which he cannot obtain. In that case he makes request of an "X," who is thought to be able to grant it. Prayer takes place when man fears something which he does not know how to avoid by his own means.

One could undoubtedly go on from there to say that man will always have desires and fears, so he will always pray. Perhaps, but let us not forget that in that case prayer does not spring from his nature but is associated with his situation. If man's condition changes, if he can satisfy his own desires, reassure himself against his own fears, he will quite simply give up prayer, which is then a poor substitute for more reliable forces, a palliative that is valueless in a precarious situation. Hence, from this point of view prayer exists only for the want of something better. The only apology we can offer when we base our reasons for prayer on nature is the popular formula, "If it does no good, it does no harm." This is prayer "on the off chance," hence in the last analysis the prayer of unbelief.

But there is more. We are said to have entered some time ago into "the era of mistrust," in the train of Marx, Nietzsche, and Freud. The mistrust obviously has fallen also upon prayer. We have finally learned that prayer is directed to anything. The God to whom we thought we were appealing is the idol of our fear, and the prayer is directed as well toward my inmost self, to "the depths." As an expression of my nature it is identical to the amulets, the fetishes, the good-luck charms. It is an instinctive means of self-defense. Its very spontaneity is precisely the thing which gives it away. To the extent to which it springs thoughtlessly from the heart, which is subject to every folly and fear, it indicates nothing more than complete uncertainty, empty pride with no real object, no true partner. If prayer is based on the nature of man, the latter has fabricated the partner out of his own nature. This is the same as saying that prayer is a word without an object and without content.

Finally, need we remind ourselves that in our day the concept of human nature has been singularly taken apart, if not completely called into question? Until a half-century ago one could hope that anything based upon nature was firmly established. That is no longer so today. One looks in vain for the *quid* of that nature, and general hermeneutics is teaching us that the human condition is in need of deciphering, of decoding, which leaves us in doubt about anything of permanence.

A Comment on Function

Yet, in the category of prayer without an object, there is another "natural foundation" for prayer, namely, that it corresponds to a constant psychological need, even in addition to our fears and hopes. It is not valid in consequence of its content, nor because it is an expression of nature, but, rather, in the degree in which it fulfills a useful function. Hence it is the act itself of prayer which is valid, irrespective of the god or absence of a god to whom it is addressed and irrespective of its content. Prayer has a cleansing and therapeutic function. Dr. A. Carrel, about 1936, developed this idea at length.* In prayer man has found a marvelous remedy against a whole group of psychic difficulties. He resolves conflicts, gets rid of guilt, overcomes negative complexes. He recovers his balance. The coming to a decision, the disposition to turn to prayer, the interior silence, the focusing for the purpose of meditation, the mere position of the body, relaxed, hands joined, knees bent, that is all beneficial to the psychic life. The very fact of talking about one's problems, of verbalizing them, of opening them up, often suffices to alleviate them, even sometimes to put an end to them. Prayer produces an obvious psychological effect. The true answer to prayer does not come from an outside power. It is already included in the act itself, for it is a question of healing. A self-therapy takes place: there is a giving up of anger and aggressiveness, a validation through responsibility and meditation, a recovery of balance through the rearranging of facts on successive levels as seen from a fresh outlook.

There is no need to enlarge upon this "utility" of prayer. All we can say is that, on the one hand, the fact is probably so. It does indeed play a therapeutic role. But that, at the same time, identifies the weakness of the position. Like all

* A. Carrel, *Prayer* (New York: Morehouse-Gorham, 1948), trans. Dulcie de Ste. Croix Wright. French edition, *La Prière,* published 1936.

therapeutic procedures it is due to be outmoded! If it is first and foremost a psychiatric procedure it is sure to be abandoned, just as surgical operations today are not performed in the same way in which they were a century ago. Man invented a remedy for certain psychic imbalances, a system of purification and adjustment, but all the remedies of our ancestors have already disappeared. Perhaps today the function of prayer can be superseded by much more effective means, and one can obtain the same results, whether by psychotherapy, or psychoanalysis or tranquilizers. The results may occasionally be more sound and sure than with prayer.

The possibility remains, moreover, that prayer might still be employed or even recommended in psychotherapy. But in that case it is an instrument which one makes use of until something better is found, and in any event it is merely a part of the over-all psychological strategy. Thus, in attributing this function to prayer, far from having given it a better foundation, far from having guaranteed its permanence and its future, one has confirmed its weakness, its transitory character. If prayer has only that therapeutic vocation, then the fact that Western man in our day no longer prays can indicate simply that he has better remedies at his disposal.

An Untrustworthy Foundation

We arrive, then, at the conclusion that the claim to establish prayer on the basis of nature or of man's need offers no trustworthy foundation, quite the contrary. I am not saying, of course, that it does not *also* correspond to a certain natural desire, a certain situation. That is obvious. But what we must keep in mind is that in making that affirmation we have not bestowed upon prayer any weight or permanence. If that is what it is, it is a passing phenomenon which we can treat as already outmoded. We cannot reassure ourselves by saying, "Of course prayer will endure always, since it is inherent in the nature of man." Nothing is more fragile. Besides, if that is what prayer is, why should we wish it to continue? Taken by itself as an expression of the heart of man, addressed neither to any thing nor to any person, a mere form of discourse, do we need to cling to prayer? Do I have any reason to be interested in it, unless I am an ethnologist, unless I am interested in making fire with flint? Taken by itself we note that it is transitory and does not carry any weight. In and of itself, of course, it has counted for something in human welfare. It has fulfilled its role, but its role appears to be on the decline. It counts for less and less, and if it is only to be considered in its relation to human nature, then there is every reason simply to render a sociological report of this decline.

If one can become engrossed in prayer it must be in the degree in which it involves another dimension. Let us say for the moment that if prayer is a kind of relation with God, then in that respect the decline of prayer takes on a greater importance, is perhaps disquieting. But that means at the same time that prayer (even beforehand) had no value by itself, that its center was not the desires, fears, and needs of man. It received its value and its content from him to whom it was addressed. Contrary to what we had been saying, it was essential to know the addressee, for the permanence of the latter is the source of the permanence of prayer. Thus the object of prayer is not a matter of indifference. To the contrary, it is essential. It is he who defines prayer, much more than the position of the body or the interior silence. Hence, in attempting to base prayer on nature we have not progressed at all. We have gained nothing. We have lost our way.

THE RELIGIOUS FOUNDATION

If prayer has no genuine foundation in nature, it would seem obvious that on the contrary it has a profound religious justification. I use the word "religious" without making the classic distinction between religion and faith, since prayer specifically is found in all religions and appears as an eminently religious act. However, I shall be content to speak only of the prayer of Christians, in as far as Christianity is *also* a religion. We are then obliged to recall some famous definitions of prayer.

Pascal

Let us consider the celebrated passage from Pascal (*Pensées,* No. 121), which says, in essence: Why God established prayer: (1) in order to communicate to his creatures the dignity of causality, (2) in order to teach us about him from whom we obtain virtue, (3) in order to make us merit virtue through work. Three essential aspects of prayer, then, are unveiled for us. God being the Supreme Cause of all, man would appear to be nothing more than an instrument. He has no genuine responsibility, since he necessarily takes his place among the effects of this first cause. He has no dignity, since he is an object. But God cannot acquiesce in that situation of his creature, whom he willed to be free, responsible, and a subject. Henceforth God grants to man the means of acting upon God, of motivating this first cause, consequently, of becoming a cause for God.

With regard to virtue, living rightly, living in accord with God, we would constantly be inclined to appropriate this virtue for ourselves, to consider it as ours, as the expression of our nature. Prayer is specifically there for the purpose of setting a limit to our pretensions, of bringing us face to face with him who judges us in such a way that we are unable to perceive any virtue of our own within ourselves. Learning from this who we are before God, and considering on the other hand what an astonishing miracle it is that there should be virtue in this fallen being, we are brought to recognize that this virtue does not come from us!

But finally, we have set out upon this path, and if God grants us virtue he does so *also* because it corresponds to a certain merit on our part. Is this a merit of good will? or of good works? or of our own righteousness? Certainly not! Here Pascal has this noteworthy formula: it is "through work." But what he means by this word is prayer itself. This diligent, resolute, untiring prayer is a work to pursue before God. It is in response to that work that God bestows virtue.

This passage from Pascal is admirable, but what can it possibly mean for man in our society? What is merit? The theological debates on that subject came to an end long ago.

Western man long ago stopped trying to acquire merits before God. What is the meaning of *virtue?* Neither the word nor the thing have any place in the mental world of our day. Virtue? Sanctimonious, bitter, sour old ladies. Virtue? That recalls grandfather's stiff collar, as he judges with an implacable eye from the height of his frame the vices of his grandchildren. Virtue? The hypocrisy of Tartuffe and of the bourgeoisie who succeeded him. That is all that modern man knows about it. To connect prayer with virtue means nothing any more.

The situation is the same, alas, for causality. In a scientific universe, causality has changed its meaning. There is no more supreme, or first, or final cause. Causality no longer depends upon outside interference, and God is no longer viewed in that way. We now know that in a world of precise compulsion we never share in the dignity of causality. At the very most we are occasionally able to utilize systems and to modify relationships. Hence, nothing is left of Pascal's meditation which carries any weight, and if that is what prayer is . . .

Barth

But let us consider what Barth says in our own day, for we might be tempted to think that if Calvin, Luther, and Pascal can no longer provide us with a foundation for prayer to move us to pray, perhaps it is merely a question of the epoch, the cultural milieu, the fashion of speech. We cannot summarize Barth's thought,* but let us call to mind

* Karl Barth, *Prayer,* trans. Sara F. Terrien (Philadelphia: Westminster Press, 1952).

two central formulas: "Prayer is the extreme case of God's grace for us" and "In prayer God invites us to live with him." God gives grace not only to save us with an eternal salvation, but also to make it possible for us to live a human life on earth. And we cannot live this human life unless we fulfill the function which God expects of man. However, we cannot assume that burden unless God is with us in tangible reality. It isn't enough for him to be with us in general, or theoretically, or that we know him abstractly. His presence must be concretized in the everyday works of life. That becomes possible through prayer, in which God allows himself to be called "Our Father," in which he really places himself within our capacity, within our reach, and one might almost say at our disposition.

Prayer is nothing more than the "God with us." It is nothing more than the self-emptying of God of which Paul speaks to the Philippians. But it is that, all of that. The existence of prayer rests upon this coming down of God, for our "to live with him" (of which it is the sign and expression) is not a divinization of man, an exalting of man. Prayer is not the form of man's transfiguration. It is the testimony of the nearness of God who comes. One understands from that how it can be characterized as "the extreme case of God's grace," for this grace is not that of a sovereign who can save and condemn, but the grace of one who incarnates it by coming to us. There can be nothing more extreme than that in God's act. Prayer is the attestation of this God with us. It is a permission granted by God that we speak to him face to face. It is God inserting man's initiative into the divine plan. It is through prayer that we are made "fellow workers for God" (I Corinthians 3:9).

By all of this we are greatly enlightened on prayer. We? Who? The person who is, if not a theologian, at least deeply committed to the Christian life and given to reflecting on revelation. But is that enough? Does that motivate a person to pray? Is there any capacity for comprehending this reality? Assuredly not! For the person living in a world without grace, with no notion of the gift freely given, who does not know what the agape can be, who is driven by our society to ever-greater conquest, gain, and possession, who respects only the tokens of power—what could that kind of prayer mean to him? Now it must be that kind of prayer, based on that principle, or it is nothing.

Doubtless the formula that prayer is "God's invitation to live with him" can seem more closely related to what we are than a dogmatic and static definition. It is "existential," and by that fact it corresponds to man in this age and culture. And yet, that is not evidence that contemporary man has a facility for prayer. Living with God is a reality which is completely foreign to him. To conceive of prayer existentially makes the definition more accessible, but not the reality. The most modern notion of prayer which is possible does not decisively change this situation. On the contrary, we are forced to admit that all these interpretations bear a stamp which is completely alien to the man of our society.

If prayer is "the center of the religious life," we have seen that that is indeed embodied in the attitude of people who are integrated into the modern religions, but such prayer has nothing in common ultimately with that which the God of Jesus Christ expects of us. It remains in the sphere of the purely human. It is not a gift. It is not a living with. It is not a sharing in the causality referred to by Pascal. It remains an act of adoration for a substitute for God. But precisely man in Western society is unable to know or receive anything but substitutes for God. That prayer in Christ is linked with the presence of the living God is a truth concerning such prayer, but that only serves to denote its strangeness, its meaninglessness, its lack of correspondence with regard to man.

The New Hermeneutic

Then could it be merely a matter of vocabulary? Can one say that, to begin with, this man is no longer accustomed to the "idea" of God, that a living God, grace, etc., are not a part of his linguistic world, and that what is being transmitted fails to get through to him for lack of terminology? Would a change of wording suffice to make prayer convincing once again, to restore the summons to pray? Surely not. One could say all one wanted to about prayer in present-day language and that would not cause people to take that prayer any more seriously. It would still remain a closed book to them, nor would they feel any more called to pray.

We might pursue the matter further by saying that it is a cultural problem, that it is man's imagery which has changed. There is, to be sure, a reality which subsists always, but the mode of interpretation of that reality is what no longer corresponds. In other words, the absence of prayer would be a question of hermeneutics. Hermeneutics of what? Of the revelation which contains the commandment, the example of prayer, and the challenge of prayer? In that case, are we to suppose that a reinterpretation, a demythologizing will incite man to pray? Here we come upon a limit to hermeneutics. It can restate the truth spoken by God in terms accessible to modern man.* It can neither render that truth more genuine and so make it easier to win a man over, nor make it capable of producing tangible results in a person's life. My impression is, rather, the contrary. Since at the conclusion of the hermeneutic operation a man finds himself caught between the classic concepts (which may mean nothing to him, but to which he is accustomed) and the new concepts (which he understands only with difficulty and at the risk of every possible misunderstanding), the operation balances out with a deficit of faith. It produces a schizophrenia of "the unfaithful faithful," a lukewarmness, a loss of interest among Christians and a frivolous, ironic skepticism in non-Christians.

But there is a second possible version of this hermeneutic, namely, a reinterpretation of the very fact that man prays. Prayer is manifested in the new religious forms (in our day Maoism, Guevarism, for example). But we have already seen the inadequacy of that fact of nature and its fundamental lack of correspondence with Christian prayer. All the hermeneutics in the world would never do away with that contradiction, that gap between this prayer which is recreated ever anew in nature and that which Jesus Christ requires of us. It cannot re-establish a connection ex-

---

* I am not entering into the debate on the problem of hermeneutics. Hence I take for granted that it is indeed possible to restate the revelation without losing it. I assume that one can find images and concepts which fit the situation of modern man, and that the latter stands in need of these, none of which is obvious.

cept on the supposition that prayer in Christ is a purely human expression of the natural need to pray. In that case one would have to make clear how it came about that that prayer exhibits completely distinctive qualities when compared with the natural desire. It is always possible conveniently to ignore these distinctive characteristics, but that only leads to a reduction of the revelation. It does not increase the possibility of prayer. This latter is not a matter of hermeneutics, whatever goal one might set for that quest.

The Inadequacy of Theology

If Western man is withdrawing from prayer, his withdrawal is not due to a change in his concepts. It has to do with the whole of life (and I do not concede that language *is* the whole of life). It is a sign of the absence of being. And here is where the basic problem lies. We shall come upon it again. Thus we arrive at the conclusion that the theological quest can provide us with excellent definitions of prayer. Theology can tell us what prayer is, can enlighten us on the meaning of the revelation concerning prayer and on the place which prayer occupies in the revelation. It can describe for us accurately "what man does when he prays." But all this comes to nothing when man does not pray. Theology cannot tell us why he does not pray, nor what needs to be done if he is to recover this "being in prayer"; nor is it able to give bearings or a sense of direction, so that man might regain the desire to pray. In the presence of the man who does not pray, theology loses its powers.

That leads us to a rather important observation. One

speaks constantly of "prayer" (and I am doing so here!), and the philosopher, the sociologist, the theologian, can make splendid statements on the subject. But we notice that that means nothing when men do not pray. In other words we need to lay hold of the fact that prayer has no existence by itself. Prayer is in no sense a thing capable of a perceptible or observable reality. There never can be anything except people who pray. That is the sole reality. One cannot speak of prayer, but only of what the person does who prays. So true is this that when a person does not pray, all the discourse about prayer simply has no meaning for him.

Hence, the search for a better terminology, a better theological explanation, can solve nothing. If prayer is to appear more genuine, urgent, and necessary, it will not be because we shall have uncovered a more solid foundation or have given a clearer explanation of the revelation. Theological accuracy can reassure us insofar as we are Christians who have entered upon the path of prayer. It can provide *us* with new reasons for praying. Hermeneutics can enlighten us concerning what we are doing when we pray, but none of that can make a nonpraying man pray.

PRAYER AS LANGUAGE

Is the crisis of prayer a matter of vocabulary? Is it linked with the crisis of language? It must indeed amount to that, since everything today is reduced to language. Quite obviously, when one prays one makes use of a certain language, words and a syntax. One talks to God as to a man.

Consequently, prayer in the first place would be dependent upon language analysis. From then on its fate would be tied to that of language. Some would even say that the study of language leads to a transformation of the style of prayer and to a renovation of its content.

Thus, by considering prayer as language, we might understand the disaffection, the anxiety, the hesitation, which hinders many from praying. They are faced with an inadequate language which expresses outmoded concepts, and even if they are not clear about it they at least sense that "something is wrong." Traditional prayer (even the nonliturgical kind which must still be something learned) is essentialist in character, and its words have no currency in an existentialist society. This is the case in a society in which existentialism is not only a philosophy but a mode of thought implied by the very situation in which man finds himself. That could be the reason why prayer is going stale and consequently is being abandoned. "It" has no meaning for modern man, but the "it" does not refer to prayer as such. The reference is to its mode of expression, its language. Now if that is the source of the indifference, then language analysis would supply the remedy: Renovate the language, or even, to begin with, just simply become aware of what the language of today means, and you can renew the enthusiasm, the vitality, the freshness of prayer.

The Problems

As in everything which concerns language, it seems to me that this point of view embraces a variety of concepts. Let us at the outset dispose of the problem of vocabulary in the strict sense of the word. That the words employed in the actions of religion, preaching, translating the Bible, prayer, liturgy, are subject to revision, that some words are obsolete and others are without modern significance—that is not serious, nor is it a matter of any great difficulty. Let us observe that for prayer, insofar as it may be spontaneous, each person can do his own renovating by using words which are meaningful to him.

It will be objected, I know, that this is impossible because the person has, from childhood on, received a certain bundle of concepts and images for this religious phenomenon which are necessarily couched in a certain terminology. (Now that the latter no longer has meaning, one gives up all participation in worship and the spiritual life because one is unable to view these through those concepts and images which one is unable to change. The rejection of the vocabulary leads to the rejection of the concepts and images, which leads to the abandonment of things spiritual, revelation, etc.) The person cannot change his terminology because he cannot change his concepts and images.

Well, I am not at all convinced by that analysis. I need only cite one example: love. The young people of today talk among themselves about love in terms which are radically new. They employ a vocabulary which they have invented, which they have forged, which is their own. They understand one another by means of this vocabulary, which they did not learn from anyone. And yet, they too have been stuffed from childhood on with images of love expressed in a certain vocabulary. That acculturation has not in the least prevented them from discovering their own vocabulary, from expressing their particular point of view, their own experience, and perhaps a renovation of the concepts of love, even if they are not aware of it.

Thus I would be tempted to say that if the crisis of prayer is a question of language and vocabulary, if prayer is language, then let the Christians manage for themselves (since it is a matter of Christians and Christian prayer). They will certainly find an adequate vocabulary, even without prior analysis and husking of concepts and syntax. But is that really the problem which faces us?

Let us do some further eliminating. By language I understand in this context the spoken language, and I shall not adopt the broader meaning that one often attributes to the term (the language of fashion, of the cinema, etc.). Prayer, as a matter of fact, largely overflows the confines of the spoken language, although this fact is often forgotten in Protestant circles. There is the prayer of incense, of bells, of the dance, of gestures. Maillot (*Vocabulaire biblique,* s.v. "Prière") is quite right in emphasizing that the words which are used to designate prayer in the Old Testament are derived from verbs implying an action: to cut (cutting oneself as an act of worship), to caress (the divine image?), to prostrate oneself, to jump. Hence, actions could have preceded oral prayer. But can one say that prayer so constituted is a language?

We are forced back upon the traditional analysis of sign, signifying, and the thing signified. That is to say, man desires to signify something by means of a certain sign. He proceeds to a sort of symbolic representation. But there remains the problem of whether or not the latter signifies anything, because for it to signify something the one who receives the sign has to know its content and what it refers to, and the thing signified must be evident to him in consequence of this. So we might say that a certain prior agreement concerning the sign is required.

Now is that the kind of action we have here? Who can say whether he to whom the prayer is addressed understands in the same way the thing that is doing the signifying? What communication does this language claim to establish? Man is the one who chose the sign, because it seemed to him to be the most appropriate one for what he wanted to symbolize. But has it any validity? In other words, does God receive it as significant? Does he perceive what is being signified *through it?* What do we know about this? And if that were not the case, then what man has chosen would not be a sign. At the very best, we can only say that we absolutely do not know whether there is communication or not. Whether the sign chosen is a sign and whether communication is established does not depend upon us.

Now it is evident that what we say along this line about religious music, or about incense, we could say just as well about spoken language. But in that case is it still possible to say that what we have here is really language? Upon what does the communication with God in prayer rest in fact? It does not rest on an experiment, nor on an interchange, nor on an equality, but on a presupposition of prior relationship. To be sure, one can always refer to matters of current concern, but the fact cannot be escaped that the traffic of prayer appeals to a past which one makes present. It requires the prior conviction, for example, that God hears. But it is a matter of faith. Such a conviction cannot be established on the level of language structure, nor on the level of communication. So we are obliged to say that prayer has no content as language, if we analyze language in terms of communication.

Indeed, one of two things must be true. Either prayer is a discourse of man, about man and addressed to man, or it is something else. In the first case it is indeed a language, but it is no longer prayer, and we are driven back to what we have already said on the subject of prayer anchored to human nature. If it has a different orientation (that is, if it is not a discourse addressed to man), then it has no content as language. The true content of prayer is not expressed in what is said, whence, among other things, the great mistake of analyzing prayer on the basis of the apparent content of the discourse, and the distinction between the prayer of petition, of praise, of intercession, etc. That sort of thing can be useful from the pedagogical point of view, but it falsifies the true nature of prayer. Vocabulary and syntax are not its specific properties.

We are reminded forcefully of this fact by glossolalia. Here we are confronted with an incomprehensible vocabulary which is not the object of any prior agreement, and with completely nongrammatical constructions. All the elements of language are lacking, to such an extent that Paul, as we know, is hesitant about the spiritual gift because it cannot be understood by the brethren who are listening to it. Of course one can suppose that it is a language for God, a special language for talking to him. On the other hand, that is not exactly the way in which the phenomenon was understood. Furthermore, what can it really mean? Does it consist of words made up by God to be put in the mouth of the person who is about to pray? That makes no sense. Hence, we have great difficulty understanding the prayer as a discourse.

But there is more. Does prayer involve communication? The moment the word is pronounced the question arises: Communication *about what,* and *to whom?* The obvious response to this second question would seem to be "God," but what does that actually mean? Of course prayer comes into existence before we can have a definition of prayer, or a precise definition of God. But can we really talk about language and about communication when the interlocutor is so indefinite, so indistinct and inaccessible that we are unable finally to say anything about him? Let us understand one another. I do not mean by that that prayer is worthless, or that it is not addressed to God, but, rather, that inasmuch as the partner is beyond our grasp and incomprehensible, it can indeed exist, but it is not communication. The latter presupposes that the two poles of the communication are defined.*

What is more, the problem increases when we consider the content of prayer. Language as communication has an

---

* In philosophical terms one might say that prayer does not involve communication. It does not transmit information. It is not an informational affair, for in it we find ourselves in the situation of *Dasein,* of "personality," the characteristic feature of which is to be removed precisely by its essence from all informative language. Thus prayer, which cannot be situated otherwise, cannot be the object of a communication analysis.

information content. If there is no information there is no language. That is where we encounter the famous (but false) question: "What can I possibly say to God? Precisely because he is God he knows all my needs, and everything I might say, in advance. There is no need for me to make a statement about anything to the Omniscient. Prayer is useless because it has no real content. If it is addressed to a true God it is a redundance. If not, then it is spoken into the void." So either it has no content of information or it is spoken into the void.

Thus we have demonstrated that prayer is not a language which makes possible the construction of a discourse. It takes place on an altogether different plane. Prayer comes to us as a decision of God, who shares his will, his power and his love with man, whom he calls upon to pray through the instrumentality of human speech. Prayer is not a discourse. It is a form of life, the life with God. That is why it is not confined to the moment of verbal statement. The latter can only be the secondary expression of the relationship with God, an overflow from the encounter between the living God and the living person.

Verbalization is not useless insofar as it is an instrument of election given to man for manifesting, to make manifest first to himself and afterward to others, that which is the essence of a living experience. Just as God proclaims his will through the voice of the prophets and apostles, within the framework of human speech, so also he requires on the part of man this rationalization of an encounter which transcends all language. But it is not my little story, my fears and desires, which I have to tell to God, as I would to an administrator or a judge. It is the statement, the proc-lamation, in all of its aspects and directions (and conse-quently including also my fears and desires!), of the life led with the living God. It is not *my* life, of which he would know nothing, but the life which I receive from him, and which unfolds in a story with him.

The Essence of Prayer

In other words, prayer is not to be analyzed like a lan-guage. It has none of that form or content, for it receives its content, not from what I have to say, but from the One to whom it is spoken. It is from the Interlocutor that this speech receives its validity. That this prayer can be what it is meant to be—a prayer—depends on him and not on me, still less on my ability to speak the adequate language. For of course I can always pronounce a discourse supposedly addressed to God. I can arrange the sentences, but it is neither the harmony of the form, nor the elevation of the content, nor the fullness of the information which turns it into a prayer. Insofar as it remains a discourse, it is in fact subject to the language analysis with which we are familiar, but that is always as discourse, that is to say, as "nonprayer."

It becomes prayer by the decision of God to whom it is addressed, but then its nature undergoes a change. Hence-forth there is a *quid* which eludes our grasp. Of course, in-sofar as it continues to be made up of words and sentences, I could pretend to treat it as language in spite of the diffi-culties emphasized above, but then we must understand that that takes place exactly in the degree in which I do not look upon it as prayer, in which that which I grasp in this manner is not what prayer is! But ultimately under those conditions I am no longer analyzing anything, since I am unable to account for the transformation which the discourse has undergone, which alters it *in its entirety.* For henceforth it is known as a prayer of Christ or as a prayer of the Holy Spirit.

That is how we should understand the famous statement of Paul, in which he says that in the last analysis we do not know what the content of our prayer should be (Romans 8:26-27), but that the Holy Spirit himself "intercedes with sighs too deep for words." This phrase has too often been interpreted as though the Holy Spirit added a little something to our prayer. In short, we pray, but not very well. Our prayer is incomplete, unsatisfactory. Fortunately, the Holy Spirit helps the situation by completing what we are unable to say. That is quite incorrect. It is the entire prayer which is the prayer of the Holy Spirit. If we conceive of prayer as language it is then that we do not know what to put into the discourse. It is nothing because it cannot have a content. Only when the Holy Spirit intercedes, and in a way which *cannot be expressed,* that is, which transcends all verbalizing, all language, then is the prayer prayer, and it is a relationship with God. *Only* then "he who searches the hearts of men knows" (hence, not by a signifying language) "what is the mind of the Spirit, because the Spirit intercedes . . . according to the will of God." We are forced to the conclusion that prayer is a gift from God, and that its reality depends upon him alone.

But if that is the case we can see the extreme difficulty of

Prayer is not a conversation

our present situation. I believe that what we have just been saying is a true account of the profound reality of prayer. What, then, can prayer mean for the man of our Western world who looks upon it purely as a discourse? This false conception is undisputed, widespread, and habitual in all the churches. Now, as long as one is living in Christian security in a Christianized society, in Christianity, in a world in which to be a Christian is *normal, correct,* and taken for granted, one can continue to pronounce such discourses. They are not prayers. The sociologist can seize upon them as a certain kind of language. We are in the domain of custom, of ritual, of spiritual hygiene. Yet these prayers go on, without result surely, because the milieu presupposes them. When the milieu changes, becomes secularized, unchurched, then one perceives clearly that these discourses make no contact with reality.

From then on one gains the impression that prayer is disappearing, but in truth it disappeared long before, at the moment when it was transformed by man into a discourse, into a purely verbal operation, into a false communication with the Supreme Being, into a misunderstanding. Man in our society cannot understand prayer except as a discourse, a sort of pious language addressed to God, a mode of communication. Every other reality is closed to him. Now precisely because prayer is not that, he cannot pray in truth. That is the tragedy.

So in the process of this analysis we have been led to discern many true components of what prayer is, and of what it is not. There has emerged progressively a "being" of prayer, which is at the same time an ought-to-be. The theological components remain true, but as we went along we were led to realize that for man in our society prayer cannot be what it is. A whole set of misunderstandings, of obsolete images, of spurious identifications, rob prayer of all further justification and being, except as a counterfeit.

3

THE REASONS
FOR NOT PRAYING

The close of the preceding chapter led us directly to raise the question of the rejection of prayer in our society. This rejection surely rests upon the lack of a foundation for prayer, which we experience and which we have analyzed. But how is this rejection expressed?

We find, on the one hand, intuitive trends which cause man to ignore prayer, and, on the other hand, we encounter rationalizations, often on the part of Christians themselves who share the difficulty of all people today and then justify themselves theologically for not praying. We leave to one side the factors making for rejection which are alleged traditionally or are simply banal.

Can one still pray when one sees clearly the lack of answers to most prayers? What significance can prayer have which is addressed to a God who decides arbitrarily what he is going to do? Is it possible to conceive of changing God's will? If he is really God, how could he modify his (perfect) decision as a result of human stammering? If he is really God, has he not already foreseen everything, including the prayer, which is then useless? If he already knows the needs of his creatures because he loves them, why petition him?

Under these circumstances, as Voltaire reminded us, "philosophers, more respectful toward the Supreme Being and less condescending to human weakness, would have reduced all prayer to resignation." Hence, to keep quiet, to resign oneself, that is the true prayer of "the enlightened man." That at least has the merit of rejecting weakness, and it is the only respectful attitude toward the God who is called "Supreme Being." It is quite true that if God is the Supreme Being, no prayer is possible! Voltaire is joined by Vigny: "To bemoan, to cry, *to pray,* all are equally cowardly."

This argument, then, has two aspects: the emptiness of prayer if God is the Supreme Being, and the promotion of Stoicism, since prayer is unworthy of man. As a matter of fact, these arguments (which, be it noted, are only the arguments of those who already reject prayer) make perfect sense from the standpoint of the twofold misunderstanding about God (the God of revelation) and about prayer. With regard to the latter, it is true that Vigny's position is justified when prayer is reduced to what Musset says about it in his attempt to show the necessity for man to pray:

If heaven is uninhabited, we offend no one.
If someone hears us, may he have pity on us. . . .

This prayer, on the off chance, obviously carries no weight, neither on the human level nor on that of God.

Let us not linger over all these well-known questions. They are too well known, simplistic, and absurd. Nor shall we dwell on the excuses so often heard, and which we ourselves indulge in: we lack time; we are overworked, rushed, harassed by everyday life in modern society. We lead a life in which every second is taken up. We haven't a moment to apply ourselves to prayer. When we relax at the end of the day we are so tired, so enervated, that we have to take tranquilizers, and concentration on prayer is out of the question. We need diversion, not an additional effort. The same is true of weekends, after having worked all week.

Does not prayer call for a certain inward peace, a certain concentration (which is impossible with the scattering effect of our work habits), a withdrawal for meditation (which is impossible with the personal involvement in our activist procedures), some free time, since prayer requires a length of time? One cannot simply plan to the second to "place oneself before God," since (especially with the telephone) we can never count on having a few moments before us. Even the fear that the telephone *is going* to ring, that someone *is going* to call us, that I shall never finish my work this evening . . . shuts the door beforehand against my entering upon meditation and prayer. And then the noise! Is not prayer first of all silence, and does not inward peace suppose a cessation of the raucous noise in this society more than in any other? We are in the midst of a continual uproar. We receive a thousand news bulletins a day, which distract us from prayer. The hubbub of voices makes meditation impossible.

We know all these justifications so well. They rest upon a mistaken point of view! Is not prayer precisely of itself peace, silence, strength, since it is a way of being with God? If we agree that prayer is indeed a sharing, which God wills to have with man, a sharing of his will, of his power, of his love, through the medium of human speech, how can we fail to see that the sole prior condition is that decision on the part of God? All the favorable psychological and sociological conditions are secondary, and may even be lacking. If prayer is a *gift* from God, then it is this gift which fulfills all the necessary psychological and sociological conditions.

In other words, it is in praying that one finds the conditions which man considers necessary. These are not prior. They are not conditions. The sorry state of modern man described above is an obstacle only for the person who has decided at the outset not to pray, because in order to pray he would have to be in the wonderful situation of Eden. But as is always the case, just at this point when God himself decides his decision suffices, even in the concrete situation, and when God gives an order he creates the conditions which, from the human point of view, are indispensable if the order is to be heard, received, and made possible.

In short, it is prayer which creates the silence needed for prayer. It is prayer which gives the time, all the time necessary, for it is a living with God. It takes us out of duration and into a different dimension (I am not referring to eternity!), in which a few seconds can have a very great time value. I cannot say to myself, "I haven't ten minutes to devote to prayer, so it is useless to try." Prayer creates its own required time. It is the prayer which restores my energies, takes away my fatigue, and which to the very end makes tranquilizers useless, for it eases every tension, every conflict.

Make no mistake about it. In writing this I am not falling back on the position I was criticizing above, that of the therapeutic value of prayer. I am not at all saying that prayer as a spiritual exercise has psychic effects (to which, moreover, it is limited), but, rather, that he to whom this prayer is addressed, in the degree in which he is a living God and whenever he speaks as creator of the conditions whereby his word is heard, modifies the psychic being in such a way that the speech addressed to him can be a true speech. It is he who makes one's youth to be "renewed like the eagle's," who takes away depression, who brings the distraught attention back into focus. From that time on, the alleged justifications are mere excuses. Is it really to the point, then, to investigate the psychological and sociological conditions of our times which appear to explain the abandonment of prayer? If God changes these conditions, if they are only excuses advanced by man, why linger over them?

But the contemporary problem is twofold. On the one hand, there is that which turns a man with this outlook away from prayer innately, and we need to inquire into the observed lack today of any desire to pray, for it is *when* a person has this desire that the Spirit works within him and prays in him.

On the other hand, man constructs his own motives for

not praying, particularly theological motives. We then have to ask ourselves, If prayer is a natural expression of man which finds new forms as fast as the former ones disappear, why does man feel the need to justify himself for not praying to the God of Jesus Christ? Is this prayer to the God of Jesus Christ something other than natural prayer? That is what seemed to emerge in Chapter 2, and that is what is now to be confirmed. Thus we could say that man in all ages has sought to escape this encounter, this prayer which is not the instinctive outpouring of his soul. He prefers by far that satisfying prayer addressed to no-one-knows-whom, but which does him good because it gives the impression that he has finally reached someone else. He prefers that to the precise prayer of Jesus Christ, which is in no sense an outpouring or mysterious. Man has always tried either to inject his natural prayer into that of Jesus Christ, or else to justify himself for not praying to the God of Jesus Christ. Since the first of these tendencies is eliminated today, there remains the second, which we must examine in its *current* form and features. Those of the past no longer concern us.

The Sociological Reasons

We now live in a desacralized, secularized, lay world, at least as far as the old forms of the sacred and the religious are concerned, for as we have already said, the new forms are sacred or religious through the nonrational: through the potential with which we invest them, through the faith which we bring to them. But in themselves they do not appear to be such. In our eyes, they do not have the givenness of something sacred and religious before which we bow. They are not consciously recognized as such by modern man. If someone were to tell him that these things are sacred to him, he would brush it off and would take it as an affront. For the person of the traditional societies, on the other hand, the sacred was an obvious and an assured fact. Hence, we cannot say that a given factor is in the category of the sacred for modern man except by an analysis of his spontaneous reactions to this or that phenomenon or institution, by detecting some resemblance between his attitude and the traditional attitude toward the sacred, then by putting together the real sacred which commands modern man's obedience without his recognizing it as such.

Secularization

With this point clarified, we can say, then, that man lives in a desacralized, lay world, and that under those conditions it is normal for prayer to disappear. Prayer in fact always implies a boundary, the recognition of a forbidden territory, a boundary by reason of the sacred or by reason of a lack of power. Prayer is the means of crossing that boundary, of making a lawful entrance (obviously by other means as well, such as sacrifices or magic) into the closed world. The sacred is, in reality, the delineation of the boundary of something forbidden, of a mystery, the establishing of a certain number of fixed points of reference, the designation of a meaning. It fades away when there no longer is a world of mystery (through science), when man claims to establish for himself other points of reference (chosen by the reason), when he puts together a meaning through some other avenue than that of myth.

Prayer is closely linked to these phenomena. Moreover, as we have noted, to the extent to which another "sacred" makes its appearance prayer reappears also, but with a quite different set of characteristics from those with which we are familiar, so that we have difficulty even recognizing it as prayer.

Traditional prayer is disappearing. That does not mean that we should regret the desacralization, the secularization. I believe that these latter are profoundly in conformity with the spirit of Christianity.* It is by a frightful corruption that the "sacred" and the "religious" have been amalgamated with the faith, on the one hand, and the Christian revelation, on the other. The sacred and the religious are always and necessarily pagan because created by man, arising out of the heart of man, answering to the needs of man. There is no greater force for their destruction than the revelation of God in Jesus Christ.

In our world man no longer experiences the need to pray. What then is disappearing? It is the instinctive, natural type of prayer, answering to man's need to appeal to a power which lies on the other side of the boundary. But instinctive, natural prayer is not Christian prayer! The Christian response to the modern rejection of prayer is not at all a matter of longing for the return of a sacral and religious world, of wishing that prayer might become simple

* J. Ellul, "La Réforme comme force de désacralisation," in *Protestantisme* (1943).

once again. That would be a completely unavailing wish, and one impossible of fulfillment. The Christian response is a matter of comprehending that prayer is something else, that it must obey another stimulus, that it must be otherwise oriented.

So modern man is no longer inclined to pray because he lives in this world. But we have to take note of the fact that the prayer which he was voicing instinctively was dictated by something quite other than the true love of the Lord. It was the old pagan formula for crossing the boundary, into which the prayer of Jesus Christ was poured as into a mold. Hence, on the one hand there is a deficiency, since modern man no longer prays and Christians are drawn into this abandonment, but on the other hand there is a clarification. We are constrained to say that if the Christian no longer prays under these circumstances, the fact is that formerly he was praying for the wrong reasons, and that his prayer entered categories which are not Christian. This should lead us to investigate what the true meaning of that prayer really is, and why the Christian, in spite of everything, might now be brought to pray. The desacralizing, the secularizing, force us from now on really to know what we are doing when we confess the faith, and when we pray.

The Climate of Reason and Skepticism

We are likewise won over by a certain spirit of realism and skepticism, realism, that is, in the colloquial sense.* To be a political realist is not to be bothered by moral

* J. Ellul, "Le Réalisme chrétien," in *Foi et Vie* (1951).

scruples. It is to trust only to power politics. It is to be interested only in natural consequences. It is to think only of "the realities," which means anything our senses and community success designate as the *only* reality, and which we confuse with the truth. Such realism implies that we are shut up in *this* world, in this society, with no other dimension or access. The important thing is to succeed here and now, and to employ every means toward that end. The end justifies the means.

To realism is joined skepticism, the refusal to believe in anything which is not concretely useful, which is not proved "scientifically," which does not enjoy the sociological support of those beliefs that this society has acquired. It is a skepticism which refuses to believe in any other supremacy, and which is expressed in a very flat rationalism. I am not, of course, characterizing philosophic skepticism, but the type which prevails in the contemporary mentality, the outlook of "plain common sense," which puts its trust in appearances and in success.

Quite obviously, skepticism and realism are two attitudes toward life which prevent prayer, but we are not obliged to distinguish in this case, as we were previously, between instinctive, natural prayer and prayer addressed to the God of Jesus Christ. The two types of prayer are equally under attack, placed in question; for as far as the Christian is concerned, realism and skepticism do not attack from outside. They have permeated each one of us. Every Christian has now become a realist in his social behavior. One need only look at the manner adopted by the "protest" within the Church to see that those who are protesting (and who certainly have good reasons for so doing, very often a genuine spiritual inspiration) adopt a realistic behavior in the worst political sense of the term.

With regard to the Christians who are not protesting, the traditional conformists, we know the dichotomy which they bring about in their lives, and the extent to which they can be just as realistic as a businessman, an intellectual, a union member, or a politician. If the Christian no longer prays, that shows the degree in which the passion for the real has won out within him over the spirit of prayer. It is because he is completely imbued with the realism of the spirit of the times (*Weltgeist*). Only an insignificant residue of prayer is able to survive. Prayer then becomes a ritual, a custom, a meaningless speech.

The same is true for skepticism. The Christian has turned skeptic even on the subject of faith. He dare not put his trust in something which is everywhere under attack. This skepticism is not the same thing as the spirit of criticism (which is necessary in connection with all statements of faith, but which should also be applied to the assumptions of the world, and to the prevailing skepticism in particular). Nor is it the same thing as natural unbelief with respect to revelation, and which continues to live within the heart of faith ("I believe; help my unbelief!"). This skepticism has none of the characteristics of that criticism and that unbelief. It is the foolish, uncritical self-assurance that one is mentally superior to all those "infantilisms" of revelation. It is the elementary easy conscience of unbelief, which supposes that it has passed beyond the stage of sinful, believing man.

This skepticism, which is instilled by all the enterprises, education, structures, opinions and value judgments of our society, dwells in the heart of the Christian, as is proved, for example, by the desperate attempt to get away from miracle and from the historicity of the Gospel accounts. That attempt, which is a temptation, wears the cloak of intellectual erudition, but its root is not that of scientific criticism. It is the poisonous mandrake-root of skepticism, which one dare not expose above ground and which, in forms employed in magic, represents the human being completely under the sway of the shrinking and shriveling of mantic operations. How could one possibly pray under those circumstances?

The Impracticality of Prayer

It is in vain that this realistic society is skeptical. It is entirely given over to doing, and to efficiency. The problem now is that we find ourselves a part of this competition of doing, for prayer has long been understood as a means of obtaining results. Doubtless that tendency has its roots in the Bible. Prayer is presented to us as having power over everything over which God has power, over demons, over sickness, over other people, over nature. It is a way of acting upon God, and over everything through him. It is power. Remember the episode of the withered fig tree. With that beginning, by reduction, rationalizing and individualizing, we have come up with a power *of* prayer. We no longer seek through prayer a conformity of our will with God's will, which makes our speech true, hence efficacious. We seek, rather, to achieve direct results, without bothering about the truth or the special will of God, or with our own obedience.

It was long ago that prayer was reduced to this level in Christianity. In a society possessed of meager means of action, always under threat of invasion by "the powers," its existence always called in question by rampaging nature or by the paucity of its resources, prayer was one means among others. The uncertain efficacy of prayer was nonetheless welcome, attractive, and reassuring in a social system lacking in efficacy. It could even appear to possess a greater eventual efficacy than all the other means. It promised, in fact, to be marvelously efficacious once God began to act. It could cure the incurable and move mountains.

But alas that attitude, far from being the attitude of faith, was diverted by the hunger for results. Prayer was taken seriously only in terms of the results which it promised to bring about. The result ultimately took precedence over every other consideration. From that moment the game was lost, *to all practical purposes*. Prayer was doomed. To be sure, those who prayed fervently in that way could congratulate themselves that the whole society was given over to prayer. What a triumph for the faith! They surely could not have noticed that *to all practical purposes* this was the foreboding of a massive setback.

One drew a boundary line between two efficacies, that of human means and that of prayer, which latter was set in motion at the point at which the human means stopped, or else it added its efficacy to the efficacy of those means. The famous saying of Amboise Paré, "I bandage, God heals," illustrates that attitude very well.

But what was to happen when the human means would

be endowed with a marvelous efficacy, when technology would truly become the key to all activity, the center of society and of the very life of man? On the one hand, the limit of efficacy beyond which prayer finally is situated has been pushed back almost to infinity, since one arrives ultimately at accomplishing *everything* through techniques. There no longer exists a fixed boundary of a *non possumus*. When something is not in fact possible by these means it is only a matter of "not yet." It is useless to pray for the healing of cancer, since "tomorrow" it will be curable. To the extent that everything is truly possible it is useless to look to the beyond for anything whatsoever. There is no other side in relation to technology. All is this side of it. Hence there is no prayer possible which would substitute for the lack of technique.

The same thing is true with respect to the efficacy which supplements human means. Technology is now endowed with an efficacy in and of itself. That is even its specific characteristic. It is not uncertain or insufficient. Today it is futile to say, "God heals," since that supposes a very great doubt about the means which we are employing. The believer, of course, faced with the triumph of his technical successes, can always say, "I owe it all to God"; but we need to be on our guard because that can belong to the category of easy talk and self-justification. It is not God who makes my automobile speed up when I step on the accelerator. Our means are perfectly consistent with our ends, and they get results which are normally, if not always, successful. Under these circumstances it is superfluous to call upon God, introducing an additional order of efficacy through prayer.

Henceforth, when modern man undertakes an operation he relies on those means which have long been shown to be effective. He does not rely on the Lord. The results he is after are perfectly obtainable without prayer. This is so with increasing frequency.

Hence prayer (the prayer which has been turned into an efficacious means) is fading out. We might even say that it is being made ridiculous by technology. One of the methods of antireligious propaganda employed in the Soviet Union is well known. Two flowerbeds were arranged at school, in which flowers or vegetables were planted. Over one of them the children prayed every day, asking God to make the plants grow, but nothing more was done with it. The other bed they watered and fertilized, etc., and observed that the plants developed much better in that one! So God was unable to do anything.

Though it is not deliberate or planned, the situation is identical in the technological society. Prayer is ridiculed because its effectiveness is entirely unpredictable, and statistical techniques are able to show that the percentage of "answers" to prayer corresponds exactly to the percentage of success which would have been the case had events been allowed to take their own course, and without prayer.

Thus we can say that in this competition prayer is doomed. But we must understand that what is doomed is that kind of prayer, the prayer of success and of efficacy, and I think that this condemnation goes much deeper than the sociological effect. In reality it is God who condemns it through the medium of circumstances. It is he who rejects the prayer turned into a means, who indicts the misconception and the abuse of that prayer. But the condemnation brought by God goes back much further than the rise of the technological society. It is from the very beginning, and man preferred not to notice.

The Confusion of Prayer with Morality

Prayer also fades out in the context of another misunderstanding, this time about Christianity as a whole. The clearest example of this is undoubtedly that given by Rousseau. In the "Vicaire Savoyard" section of *Émile* Rousseau writes on the subject of prayer. The argument runs: What am I to ask him (God) for? All I ask of him is the ability to do good. Why ask him for what he has given me? Has he not given me a conscience for loving the good, my reason to enable me to know it, freedom to do it? If I do evil I have no excuse. I do it because I will it. To ask him to change my will is to ask of him what he asks of me, is to want him to do my work.

This remarkable analysis corresponds very well to the notion of a Christianity reduced to morality, in which prayer is narrowed down to putting into practice the power to fulfill a duty. If it is actually a matter of carrying out a "good," if everything boils down to a morality, then it is true that prayer makes no rational sense. To state the problem in that way is precisely to acknowledge what Rousseau is emphasizing, namely, our freedom to choose between good and evil.

But if man is thus free, if he is not inclined to evil by any special force, then it is true that he has no reason to pray.

He is endowed with all that he needs for doing good, and prayer would only be a means of not putting his ability into practice, of running away from his responsibilities. That is precisely what he cannot do since his will is his own. That he be rightly occupied depends on him. Rousseau's position on the subject of prayer is entirely consistent. In other words, when one reduces life to a series of ethical decisions, when one reduces Christianity to a morality, then prayer has no place. That in fact is what has come to pass and been made clear. The decline of prayer is evidence of this decline with regard to the faith.

Conversely I must realize that if I pray I signify and attest by that very act that I am inclined to evil, that my nature is incapable of carrying out the good, that my will is not free, that my reason is defective in that area, that my conscience deceives me. More than that, in the act of praying, I am signifying that the good is not an objective reality known in advance, with evil as an equivalent opposite, as though I had a choice to make between two things. I am signifying that, to the contrary, evil is a condition, a situation which affects me, and that it is not visible to the eye like a tumor in healthy flesh. I am signifying that the good is not a source for objectifiable commandments, but that the good is the will of God. Even if I am not a theologian, that is what I mean when I pray.

These are ideas which are especially obliterated. Good, evil, morality, the will of God, all that is now being interpreted in Rousseau's way. And even if I am not a theologian, even if I am incapable of formulating the problem as Rousseau formulated it, I know it, I sense it, I see it, because that is what the society in which I find myself is constantly broadcasting. Apart from logical reasoning, without any attempt at intellectual consistency, I draw instinctively (without knowing *whence* I am drawing it) the same conclusion that Rousseau drew. Hence, in actual practice, I stop praying about the right action which I am to perform, just as I give up praying about effective action.

The Breakdown of Language

Finally, in this sociological sphere there is another decisive factor to be underscored. If prayer is not the transmission of information, it is above everything else a speech. Human speech becomes invested by God with a new magnitude, a dignity, a meaning. One can, in fact one must, then say that whatever affects human speech affects prayer. Now it is easy to see where we are in the technological societies. We are in the midst of a tragic crisis of language, in which words can no longer attain the level of speech.

This is due to a hundred causes which we cannot analyze here. Let us merely note the existence of the crisis, which boils down to the absence of a subject and the absence of a hearer. The current, extreme movement of language analysis leads us to look upon language as having a veritable autonomy. Man, in this connection, is no longer anything but a mouthpiece. It is not really the person who is speaking. What is spoken is the language itself, for it gets its meaning, content, syntax and structure from a social context. It is one structure among others, and as a structure it functions of itself. When I speak, I have the illusion that I am saying something. That is an illusion, for it is not I who speak, but the language through me. I must not say, "I am talking," but, "It is talking." There is no subject in this operation, and likewise he to whom the discourse is addressed is not a Thou. He, too, becomes part of a system of communication. There no longer is a fellow being in the language relationship. There are only two agents of a functioning structure.

If this extremely negative analysis has some appearance of truth, that derives from the situation of actual fact, the absence of encounter in our society, the absence of I and Thou, because man tends to make himself into a thing in the universe of things in which he finds himself placed. But if that is what language has become, it is no longer the bearer of a message (a kerygma) but only of a communication. Likewise, the words which I pronounce cannot become speech. For there to be a message, or a speech, the person of the speaker must come into play the moment he speaks. A person-to-person relationship must be established. But we are told that language is not that—I would be inclined to say is *no longer* that. The speaker has nothing to say for himself and the person addressed can receive nothing of himself. It is impossible to progress to the stage of speech which is lived, dynamic, new, evocative. Where is speech to be found under these circumstances? Nothing has content any longer.

How can one still pray? The language whose structure is under analysis cannot be the carrier for prayer, and in that case how can it be employed either as speech to God or as word from God? We live with the bitterness of a prayer which is impossible because understanding is impossible.

It does no good to have an intellectual knowledge of this analysis of language, or to draw sociological or philosophical conclusions from it. What we are referring to here is the expression of a lived reality, and the person who lives it, even if he can have no formal concept of it, by that very fact lives the flaw affecting all prayer, feels the futility of the words he is pronouncing, and in this world of tense news coverage does not know where to place a prayer which would be anything other than a televised monologue. This sterilization affects the deep sources of prayer, and we are living in a time of great discouragement and confusion, faced with the sorely tested futility of our words, which are dissipated without being able to become speech.

THE THEOLOGICAL JUSTIFICATIONS

As is so often the case, theology comes in to justify a fact already established, to ratify it, to show us that it is indeed in conformity with the will of God.* Thus we have a right to theological explanations to tell us that prayer actually has no meaning or value, or perhaps to put us in such a position that prayer serves no purpose. These are two aspects of current theological activity. In all these theological efforts we discover that the source and point of departure is the bad conscience of the Christian with respect to science, the increased value accorded the achievements of modern man, the anxiety to keep up with our modernity, an exaggerated view of the self. All these attitudes were well known

---

* The latest example of this justifying surrender of theology to fact is provided by the hermeneutic of J. M. Robinson.

to the biblical writers and had already been found worthless, but they keep coming back constantly into the mind of the religious person. Today we are witnessing a new theological offensive in that direction.

Man Come of Age

We shall not analyze all the evidence. Two examples alone will suffice. An entire school of thought is teaching us today that prayer is in large measure unacceptable,* and one can examine that on two levels. Why has man always felt the need to pray? Through a natural bent of his soul? Because God placed the need in his heart? Because prayer is speech? Not at all. It is simply that man was living in an economy of scarcity. Goods were hard to come by. It was difficult to meet one's needs. Man was accustomed to want. Plenty was an exceedingly rare occurrence, so that man was obliged only to *hope* for it, and he always more or less took the attitude of a beggar. He stretched out his hand for someone to have pity on him. He expected compassion to give him the next day's sustenance. The beggar expects it from the passerby. Man expected it of God.

Thus he had a false image of God, brought about by his economic situation, and he established a false relationship with him. Now, in a society of abundance, we no longer need to beg, to expect something from God in a supernatural way. We can re-establish a true relationship with God with a more accurate concept of him. He no longer is the Great Dispenser of favors. We no longer need to be favored. We

---

* E.g., Father Cardonnel, *Dieu est mort en Jesus Christ* (1968).

no longer need anything dispensed to us at all. We are not dependent upon God materially and out of necessity.

This brings us to the other level. Prayer was bound up with an infantile relationship with God and with a paternalistic vision of him. In prayer man acts like a little child afraid to accept his responsibilities, and who looks to a grown-up for order, advice, and protection. He does not feel that he is doing right unless he is obeying (instead of assuming his own responsibilities). Prayer puts us in the position of a minor with respect to God. It cuts us down, not to the form of the little child which Jesus commands us to be, but to the stage of infantilism. It establishes our relationship with God on a basis of paternalism. We are not grown up enough to act by ourselves. We take refuge in irresponsibility, in vacuity, in indecision. We put the decision-making off on God, etc.

That is not what God wants of man. To the contrary, he wants people who have come of age, who are responsible. But precisely in our day, and as a result of technological progress, we have come of age. We can assume our responsibilities and accomplish everything ourselves. Thus, under these conditions, we have no further need to pray. What one used to ask for in supplication, man can now acquire for himself. In other words we encounter again what we were describing above in connection with the increase of technological means, but now, instead of treating the situation simply as a fact, the theologian welcomes it as something good and as a spiritual progress.

What does this progress consist of? A new, a more "true," concept of God, that is, one of Jesus Christ alone, and no longer one of a transcendent Father to whom man yields, before whom he sees his own guilt, before whom he becomes a minor. Jesus Christ is true God *because* a brother. He has no superiority in relation to people. He does not pretend to judge or to command. He is true because he treats people as "friends," as equals, and he does not put them on a lower level. It is useless to pray to this brother. Moreover, we do not meet this Jesus Christ in the clouds or in a transcendence. Precisely because he wants *only* to be a brother we meet him in our brothers. God in Jesus Christ is found in one's neighbor. That is why the two commandments are identical. That is also why prayer does not mean much, because with regard to our neighbor we are not called upon to petition but to give. Such is the new relationship which is theologically more correct, according to this school.

The true is that which is described for us in the parable in Matthew 25, and we see that there is no place in it for prayer. So it is a matter of giving to others, and that mature, virile attitude corresponds to a society of abundance, hence to the new, factual situation of man. But the new concept is at the same time more accurate theologically on the subject of man as well. Man having come of age has acquired human dignity (and the Pope felt it necessary to declare that this dignity was a new aspect, which is theologically accurate to such a degree that one could write that this dignity is the image of God). But this dignity implies that man stands on his own feet, that he is not submissive, that he does for himself and does not petition, that he establishes righteousness (and not charity), that he organizes in conformity with the vocation to which God called him in Genesis (one no longer takes into account the break with God), that he is himself the cause of events (and has no further need of receiving the dignity of causality from God), that he directs himself (without reference to a superior), that he assumes his responsibilities, that he obeys nothing and no one.

Such is the dignity of which the theological validity is being proclaimed, the dignity of man who was made only slightly inferior to God and who should dare to be what God wills him to be. Hence we reject all the humiliations and accusations with which the Old Testament and the Epistles belabor man. Is this man, then, completely independent of God? "Yes, and that is good, for now if he serves God he does so freely. He is bound to God by a genuine love, now that all the self-interest has disappeared. He no longer expects or hopes for anything from God, so the relationship is purified." Obviously under these circumstances there no longer is any question of a fear of God (which biblically was the beginning of wisdom—but, we are told, that was an image connected with scarcity and the authoritarianism of the father!), nor of obedience, nor of prayer, since there is nothing to be received from God, hence nothing to ask him for.

Of course we must be aware of the fact that this majority (so called) of mankind which has become adult (so called) in our time corresponds to a certain reality, the results of which are clearly visible. Our society is no longer characterized by prayer but, rather, by the assertion of rights. From the standpoint of human relations I could even assert that that is one of its principal characteristics. We are in an age in which the spirit of prayer is replaced by the spirit of de-

mand. We think that to request something of someone po-
litely (or in prayer) is a humiliation. The great act of prayer
is now understood as an attitude of inferiority. To get down
on one's knees is to accept an inferior position.

This is true when the relation is a direct one between
man and man in the absence of a third party, but there
ceases to be any inferiority when between these two men
there is a third party, God. Those for whom humiliation is
a problem are those who reject the possibility of God as the
third party, the third person, the indispensable witness to
our relationships, he without whom the human relationship does not exist at all. If we assume there is no relationship except that of horizontal otherness, if we refuse to see
anything else than the Thou of the other person, then prayer
actually has no place. It would turn into an alienation
(J. A. T. Robinson). But if we believe in the effective presence of the Lord when we encounter the other person,
whom we see in Christ and for Christ, how could there be
a humiliation in the act of prayer?

How could one suppose that there is humiliation in the
fact that God is God? We cannot help recalling the dignity
of many Moroccan beggars who feel no humiliation in asking alms because they depend upon God, because their prayer
addressed to the passerby is backed up by a prayer for God
to give reserve, dignity, serenity, and independence. God is
the intermediary between the two men, the one who begs
and the one who is accosted, the one who gives and the one
who receives. It is he who assures to each his dignity.

But that fact is no longer acknowledged, nor do our the-
orists recognize it for what it is when it is encountered.
They construct abstract, schematic human relations which,

without taking stock of the real, assume on principle that it is humiliating to beg alms, that to pray to anyone at all is an act of immaturity, etc. The consequence is that human relations now have become relations of suspicion, of defiance, of mistrust, of contempt and, in the extreme case, of violence. This latter is manifestly a mark of superiority and worthy of the adult human being! Having rejected prayer, one can no longer set up any relationship but that of force, in the triumphant pride, to be sure, of proclaiming the commonplace, "We are not asking for charity but for justice," justice being the demand that my desires be satisfied in some anonymous manner. For having rejected prayer, modern man is permeated with the feeling of jealousy, which goes by the name of maturity! However that may be, and without noticing the predictable consequences, the theologian congratulates himself on the progress. He explains how it is that this corresponds exactly to the will of God. With respect to the human being whom sociology describes for us as man in a technological society, theology assures us that it is *good* and *lawful* that he be what he has become through circumstance. This is a theology of justification which takes a cheap view of prayer and also of the fatherhood of God. The two go together.

The Death of the Father

It goes without saying that this attitude requires putting to one side or abandoning a great many biblical passages. But that does not embarrass our theologians, who are skillful at picking and choosing. One of the most crucial passages is the parable of the prodigal son.

There we see a son who conducted himself without any dignity. To be sure, his first act was "valid." He wanted to break loose from his father and to determine his own destiny. When he claimed his portion of the inheritance he was behaving like an adult human being. But afterward he returns in a sorry state. He humiliates himself, gets down on his knees, begs for pardon. What degradation! Here we have precisely an example of those prayers which "indicate degradation." It surely was not when he was wasting his money that he was degraded, but when he came to beseech his father. What is even more telling is that the parable (which of course was never put forth by Jesus in that form) seems to disapprove of his departure and to approve of his humiliation. It is typical of the bourgeois* morality.

And the father! He is typical of the paternalizing of relationships. It is he who keeps all the goods. It is he who acts as "the great lord" on the return of his son by giving him a robe and a ring, and by having the fatted calf killed for him. This is an attitude which is humiliating for the son, who has no way out but to ask pardon, and who receives a certain gift in place of what is due him! The paternalizing is even more marked toward the older son, who is under his father's orders, who has no right to protest, and who is silenced when he does protest, in spite of the fact that he works continually for his father without wages of any kind.

This parable is unacceptable. It is merely a reflection of the paternalistic structure of the society of that day, justi-

---

* The adjective "bourgeois" occurs in a number of writings setting forth this opinion. I have always wondered what could have been the bourgeois mind in the time and milieu of Jesus Christ.

fying as it does that system of relationships in which the superior does not (because of the structure) respect the personality of the inferior. It is an unacceptable parable clearly expressing a situation of scarcity. The younger son, poorly paid, then out of a job, without any dignified means of sustenance, is bound to his father, and for that reason is obliged to humiliate himself. Similarly, the patrimony is entirely in the hands of the father for the simple reason that one is in an economy of scarcity. It is an unacceptable parable in which the relationships are still those of favor, of pardon, of prayer, instead of being based on independence, pride, autonomy. Unacceptable prayer. . . .

Starting with that hermeneutic of prayer as an expression of an economy of scarcity, we have been led to consider the relationship with the Father. But here we come upon a final aspect of this theological movement (indirectly, for such is not its purpose) which justifies the abandonment of prayer. There lives within us all the necessity for the "Death of the Father." Haunted by words and imagery derived from a cheap Freudianism, we take it for granted that a child does not become a man until he has killed his father,* and from there we fall effortlessly into the theology of the death of God. We shall not, of course, enter into an analysis and account of what these (quite diverse) theol-

* To all those who hold forth on the subject I reply that I would prefer a little more courage, and that I cannot take this business seriously unless there is a real, bloody murder of the father. All the rest, this putting father to death in mental pictures, in speech, by contempt, etc. reflects cowardice, mediocrity, baseness of soul.

ogies are. They are entirely explained by the circumstances, and are purely and simply a reflection of the concept alluded to above, and of the consensus of our society. It is good that sociology should report it for us, but that theology should take it to its credit is ridiculous.

Yet we must understand that this theology (as well as the sociological and psychological reality which it expresses, explains, and justifies) necessarily raises the question: To whom could one pray? God is dead. To what shall my prayer be addressed? God is no longer a person. How then am I to talk to him? With this outlook, prayer has absolutely no further meaning. It even has no being, since it derives its validity from the one to whom it is addressed. But there no longer is anyone to whom to address it. It is a speech into the void, perhaps a talking to oneself (how could it be a prayer?), a speech thrown into the wind! How is it still possible to express something if we know that "heaven" is empty, and that only Nothing is God?

For let us not be deceived when it is said that only a certain image of God is outmoded, that in this theology it is merely a matter of noting that man can no longer believe in a concept of God which was created in another cultural setting and whose terminology and expressions no longer mean anything in our culture. Under their seeming wisdom and intelligence these statements conceal something quite different.

If one rejects the idea of God as a principle for explaining the universe, well and good. But immediately we notice that it is the Creator who is called into question, a concept looked upon as relative to a prescientific age. The creation was a pure myth which had for its purpose to account for the existing world. If one rejects "the God who is" as an outmoded idea, well and good. But if he "is" not (to be sure we must not confuse being with the problem of existence), then what is it which Is? I know that this will be taken as an essentialist attitude, but if he is not, how in any case is one still to pray? To say that God is "neither substantive nor substance," that again is well and good. But to come up with these innumerable "definitions" today: God as Ultimate, as Depth, as Structure, the creating Ground of our existence, the goal of our social life, the source of our historic existence, etc., reveals the limitations and value of this theology.

It is a renewal of the experiment of Bauer and Feuerbach, namely, faced with a given stage of science, to try nevertheless to recover God, and to make him acceptable to that science by acknowledging his death as a precondition for this consideration of him. But in so doing one arrives at a "definition" which is entirely abstract (more so than the dogmas of the Trinity). One submerges oneself in a purely speculative theology, in a system of thought which looks scientific but which is in fact imaginary as a result of the rejection of the biblical text. This latter becomes a needless, though occasionally useful, reference, completely permeated by a volatile, shapeless spiritualism, lacking ultimately in any reason for existence.

Under such circumstances one can surely conclude that this theology is not going to bring any great results. It does not reach traditional Christians who, whether one likes it or not, remain attached to concepts which for them are not outmoded. It holds strictly no interest for non-Christians. It is a great illusion to suppose that one will reach the unbeliever by that path. The failure of Bauer and of Feuerbach should teach us that the unbeliever will unconcernedly select from these thought-forms whatever tends to confirm him in his unbelief, and in his rejection of the reality as well as of the truth of God (however one might formulate these for him).

The remainder of the statement does not interest him at all. Investigations and reflections of that kind might stir a few intellectuals to thinking about it. From then on, why worry? For the simple reason that the theology of the death of God puts on a great theatrical display. In various of its shock-forms it is broadcast by the mass media, and if that is the case, make no mistake about it, this means that the death of God, as copyrighted by the theologians, is a "shock-headline," carrying out the Golden Rule of "blood on the front page." It is a "human interest" story like the death of the Pope, the moon walk, the war in Biafra. Through the medium of this picture-making, the believer is perplexed. His faith is called in question, his hope frustrated. Of course it is good that the mere conformism of faith be jolted, but is it good to do that by means of a news flash, with its misconceptions and hollow statements? We shall go no further.

For the Christian who is not a theologian, what is left is an embarrassment and an uncertainty which paralyze prayer. If God is nothing, if one can hope for nothing from him, what should I pray? What is there to say to this Inaccessible? What cry into the void? What good is it, since it is not true, not actually true, that man has spoken and can still speak face to face with God as friend with friend? A taste of ashes and bitterness fills the mouth about to give itself to prayer. This bitterness dare not be expressed—on whose account?—and these ashes stifle the cry. Now that God no longer exists, the joining of the hands becomes a sinister farce, and to speak is nothing but a monologue in front of the mirror.

If that is how the simple faithful who do not understand clearly can feel about it, I am not at all sure that the intellectual and the theologian would not also be paralyzed in their prayer by this theology of the death of God. Even when one has an understanding of this or that aspect, how can one avoid being overtaken by doubt and tempted to keep silent? If society is everything, what good is it to talk to anyone except my neighbor, and what shall I say to this society? The vacuity, the uncertainty, the intellectualism, the lack of depth bring me to sterility in prayer. In that case the pastor can well say, "Brethren, might we perhaps try to pray?" It has become so futile, so difficult! And one could even say, "Why try?" There is nothing, after all, but a speech broadcast into space, or which comes back to me again, a speech with no recipient, and one which I know is dead as soon as spoken. Why should it leave my lips?

If I know that "death of God" does not mean what it is currently assumed to mean, I am, even so, overcome by perplexity just when I am at the point of speaking, and I never manage to escape from this prior question, "What about the death of God?" Then my prayer dries up of itself, unless, perchance, it becomes *purely* spiritual. That is indeed the temptation of this theology, a prayer which remains unarticulated, very ardent perhaps, but without content. There is not even a thought of saying the "Our Father," of appealing to a *Father*. Heaven is nonexistent. The being of God is an error. The *Name* is merely a cry, an interjection without content, and sanctification is an outworn ritual. Yes, it is purely spiritual, without sentences and without concepts, without references and without interests, but full of love and fervor.

Then what prayer do we recognize by these terms? For we do recognize it! It is an old acquaintance. It is the prayer of the mystics, the plunge into the vast silence, into the ineffable, into the incommunicable. If the theology of the death of God does not wish to remain a purely intellectual system, completely dried up, if it would retain any spiritual content, it can only end in pure mysticism.

But what about the person with no temperament or taste for mysticism? Of course his situation is eased somewhat, for he simply finds himself confirmed by theological doubt in his sociological disinclination to pray. Everything in our society invites him to neglect meditation and to sidestep prayer. He has no desire to pray. At no time does he feel disposed to it, and the less he prays the harder it is for him to do so. There is a certain embarrassment, a certain fear of remorse lest, having neglected prayer, he might again be found in the presence of that God. But fortunately theology rescues him. He will not in any case be in the presence of anything or of anyone. He will only be confronted by a word, by a manner of speaking. That is all.

Thus the new theology, far from discovering an urge to combat the sterilizing power of this society, to overcome the sociological dullness, to demolish the system, to desacralize the activism, with a view to making a place for peace and for prayer, finds confirmation for everything which turns one away from prayer. That "little candle stub which is still smoldering"—theology carefully extinguishes it. The smoke annoys us. The slightly broken reed, which the new theology would have us cut off entirely. After all, the place should be kept clean.

What a marvelous cleansing by means of the absolute void, in the name of honesty and authenticity! Nothing will be left (least of all prayer), except a virile unconsciousness. Everything will be well disinfected. In texts which are indeed outworn, that was called sweeping the house, putting it in order by casting out a little demon hiding in the corner. It was also called whiting the sepulcher in order to avoid identifying the corpse.

4

THE ONLY REASON
FOR PRAYING

In the actual situation in which Western man finds himself we can supply no demonstration of the necessity for prayer, or even of its usefulness. It is futile to pretend that prayer is indispensable to man. Today he gets along very well without it. When he does not pray he lacks nothing, and when he prays it looks to him like a superfluous action reminiscent of former superstitions. He can live perfectly well without prayer. The proof is complete. No one can demonstrate to him that he really needs it although not realizing it, nor that he would be so much better off if he prayed. There is no reason, no proof, no motive to be invoked.

This situation, which is that of everyone, is also that of Christians, in spite of appearances. We in the churches are caught in a contradiction. On the one hand, there is a manifest drying up of private prayer. People read the Bible less, meditate less, and pray individually less and less. We are oriented toward a community action or manifestation of the Christian life. We seek a community of faith, of expression, and of service. The Christian life is conceived more and more as a community affair, but that precisely minimizes the role of personal piety. On the other hand, there is a growing mistrust of liturgies, of collective prayers and rites, a feeling of invalidity in public prayer, of the difficulty of truly praying together. As a result, prayer is in effect questionable in both of its aspects. Man has no further reason to pray.

Of course, one can then ask: But do you have to have *a reason* to pray? Must one search for motives? That line of argument is in fact purely theoretical and intellectual. Am I really going to pray because I have a reason which is rational, clear, explicit and conscious? Am I to pray because . . . ? Must prayer have a cause? Prayer is a spiritual act, and I should accept it and live it as such. Since it is a spiritual act I do not need proof, nor do I need to look for reasons. I pray, or I do not pray. There is the superabundance of faith to be expressed, and if that is not present then all the proofs and motives in the world will not make me pray. Possibly with motives I might force myself to put together some words of prayer, but am I going to make myself pray? Will it be a true prayer if it is forced? Prayer is an experience. It rests on the lived and living contact with the Lord, and anyone who has had that experience knows how important prayer is. It suffices to try it out, for prayer is that kind of thing. It is not a matter of the intellect.

That is all perfectly true, but we cannot forget the person who has not yet had that positive experience, or who has even had a negative experience with prayer, a sense of confronting the void, or an absence and a failure of answers. We cannot forget the modern criticism of spiritual experience, whether it be, with Barth, a tendency to objectify all reality or, with the new theology, the rejection of the experience as a basing of the Christian life on the past, with theological error as a consequence. We also are witnessing a rejection of the experience of sin and of repentance (which are looked upon as concepts productive of rigidity), or of prayer (which is treated as an illusion). Finally, we have to take into account the actual situation of modern man, which we have been considering.

Faced with the spiritual laziness and lukewarmness, with the errors and rationalizations which have been brought about in the lives of all Christians as well as in all the churches, we know that God in Scripture comes to our aid with his command: if you live by the Spirit, then you go beyond the commandment. You are fulfilling the will of God. You are entering into the experience of the reality, of the truth, of all the spiritual rudiments.

That is all well and good, but in these times of dryness, of hardening, of morbidity, of despair, of alienation, of negation, of disobedience, of rejection, when there is nothing left "in our hearts" which tells us to "seek his face," when the barriers and misunderstandings are accumulating between God and me, when I am precisely unable to act like the younger son in the parable, that is to say, to return to the Father, when I am ashamed to come back, and I let fear and remorse pile up between God and me which make a return seem impossible, when everything turns me away —where shall I find again any inward fervor, any enthusiasm for prayer?

No, at those times I have in fact to cling to "a reason" outside myself, objective, which I find compelling, which pushes me along in other words, like a hand in my back forcing me ahead, constraining me to pray. It is the commandment which God in his mercy has granted to make up for the void in my heart and in my life. "Watch and pray"; that is the sole reason for praying which remains for modern man.

The Commandment

We must be clear about the meaning of the term "commandment." Although since Barth the distinction is quite well known, it might not be entirely beside the point to remind ourselves of the contrast between law and commandment. Law is always objective, universal, neutral, impartial. It has a sort of independent existence. The law is established over against me. I am a stranger to it. It relates to me externally. It is present as a gauge against which I can measure every one of my actions, like a cold requirement which hangs over me under all circumstances. It is like a constraint which does not break my will but which does away with it by requiring in its objectivity even a complete submission. The law is an object, external to my life. It takes no account of the circumstances in which I find myself. It is perfect and serene. My death, my bitterness, my weakness and vanity, make no difference to it at all.

The commandment is the reverse of all that. It is a personal word addressed to me. A commandment is always an individualized word spoken by *him* who commands to *him* who should obey. It expresses the will of the superior, yet in addressing itself to a person in his individuality it takes into account the circumstances in which he finds himself, the human reality. It is always formulated *hic et nunc*. It is always a circumstantial word, which is never a sort of permanent, eternal presence, even when it is God who formulates this commandment. It is always registered in terms of the concrete facts, and must necessarily be interpreted in relation to them. It is a person-to-person relationship.

To be sure, the law can be transformed into a commandment. It can depart from its icy majesty to accost a particular person in his life. In a sense, the Jews must have experienced this transformation, as is evidenced in Psalm 119. And in Jesus Christ we have the fulfillment of the law, one aspect of which is precisely that it is no longer law at all, but entirely commandment.

But the worst mishap is the transformation of commandment into law, the objectification of the word of God, or the legalistic interpretation of the commandment. What is spoken by God to man in biblical history, a holy history of the walking together of God and man, cannot be transformed into a law which is valid of itself and universal. Everything depends upon the commandment's being "made real in the present" (not by our efforts and our hermeneutical methods), that is to say, upon the commandment's being received now as real and personal by each one in his own heart. The pronouncement, the proclamation of the commandment must be heard afresh, received as a new word spoken for the first time, by which God is speaking to me, and as something which I *must* now do.

For it is indeed a question of a duty expressed in a summons. I am called by the very setting forth of the commandment. The order is not of force in and of itself, but as a summons which puts me completely into relationship with the one who is calling upon me. When I hear that word I am not left untouched, with a free will capable of entirely independent decision. The command given me already starts me off in a certain direction. Yet for it to exist I still have to receive it for what it is, for the living commandment which concerns me.

The summons of the commandment is contained in its entirety in the Bible. But it does not cease to be a word for being "written" (hence objectified). It does not become letter, nor does the commandment become law. The word inscribed in the Bible is always living, and is continually *spoken* to him who *reads*. Thus the commandment to pray is constantly renewed. Throughout all ages it is said to each person, "call upon me in the day of trouble; I will deliver you, and you shall glorify me" (Psalm 50:15); "Watch and pray that you may not enter into temptation" (Matthew 26:41); "Watch at all times, praying that you may have strength to escape all these things that will take place, and to stand before the Son of man" (Luke 21:36). Thus does Jesus command, after having drawn attention to the signs of the end of the age; and Paul, in the midst of ethical injunctions, writes, "Admonish the idle, encourage the faint-hearted, help the weak, be patient with them all. See that none of you repays evil for evil, but always seek to do good . . . pray constantly, give thanks in all circumstances; for this is the will of God in Christ Jesus for you. Do not quench the Spirit" (I Thessalonians 5:14-19). So prayer indeed rests upon a command. To give thanks is the will of God for us.

Can we fail to see that these words, which appear to us to be addressed to others and to belong to a time so long ago, concern us personally and are actually a commandment, since the situation they refer to is always my situation? Am I to be exempt from temptation, first of all that of sleeping when Jesus is in agony? There is the temptation of indifference, of loss of zeal, of alienation, and the temptation to give up on myself. Will I be exempt from distress, from agony, from misfortune, from despair?* On those occasions should I not remember Psalm 50, and the word which has become personal to me because I am suffering? Am I to be exempt from the call to support the weak and comfort the poor, to be careful not to repay evil for evil? But if I accept that as the meaning and content of a human life, how can I carry it out unless I pray?

* "The best disposition for praying is that of being desolate, forsaken, stripped of everything" (St. Augustine). That is what is restored in the contemporary situation of prayer.

To have assumed the duty, to have become responsible, inevitably makes me subject to this commandment of prayer, without which the duty can never be rendered in truth (it might be materially) and the responsibility can never be assumed. Will I remain unscathed in the trials of the end of the age? Am I not surrounded by wars and rumors of wars, by the clash of nations, by anger and threats? Will I be immune to the daily wear and tear? Can I not have a "heart weighed down with excess of eating and drinking" (overconsumption!), by the cares of life (overwork and excess productivity). All of that in reality describes my state, my life at every moment. So, bound to such conditions, in such a situation, how can I fail to accept the command of prayer as a commandment which touches me in my situation? The identity of condition and state of life means that the word spoken to someone else in another age is really spoken to me now.

When Jesus says that under these circumstances prayer alone makes it possible to be a man, to "look up and raise your heads" (Luke 21:28) and to be seen standing before the Son of man; when we are told that, far from being a resignation, a collapse, a neglect of responsibility, prayer is to the contrary that which opens the way to being fully man, truly responsible, and that *without prayer* in this situation a person can only demean himself, give way to his fear, to his egotism, to his delirium; how in that case can I fail to accept it as the most *personal* of the commandments, since it shows me the only way to be a *person*. It is a way which is contrary to what I can rationally suppose or analyze, but just because this word contradicts me, it in fact summons me.

That is the perspective in which we should receive the command to "pray without ceasing," for under these circumstances prayer is not a casual exercise which one can shake off with a few moments of meditation. To the extent to which it is, as we have seen, bound up with all that is most eventful (threats, accidents, wars) and at the same time that which is most continual (suffering, responsibility), it belongs to the totality of my life without any loophole, from the most superficial to the most decisively profound, from my moral obligation toward others to my participation in an affluent society. Thus prayer is not an affair of the moment. It is the continuous woof on which is woven the warp of my occupations, my sentiments, my actions. The warp without that woof will never constitute a whole, a pattern, and the tissue of life will never be woven. We will, in fact, give way to every solicitation. Without prayer we are like children carried away by every wind of doctrine.

What are we to say of the most profound of all? We know the parable of the widow who importunes the judge to see that justice is done her. One must be careful at the beginning and at the end of the passage (Luke 18:1, 8). The evangelist states that Jesus spoke this parable "to the effect that they ought always to pray." Hence it is indeed a question of prayer. Yet oddly (in such a strange way that many commentators detach this sentence, saying that it is a separate *logion* inserted here somewhat by chance) the account ends with *two* conclusions, or, rather, with one normal conclusion and one interrogation which seems unrelated: "will not God vindicate his elect who cry to him day and night?" So ends the exhortation not to slacken in prayer.

But immediately: "when the Son of man comes, will he find faith on earth?"—an apparently unnatural question in this context. Now it is just this interrogation which seems to me to relate directly to the commandment of prayer. That is the true, crucial responsibility. The satisfying of justice which is in question in the parable does not have to do with social justice, or with legal justice, or with my being protected from those who wish me evil. It is the final, the crucial justice, the justification of the person, peace in God, the kingdom of God, the sun of righteousness shining upon all things. Prayer has a decisive role in that triumph, for it will be the answer given by God.

But this prayer must continue to be maintained, and there is nothing to ensure that, since it can only be a prayer of faith. Nothing guarantees its duration, its continuance. That is what Jesus is saying to us in this interrogation. Thus vigilance is in fact linked with prayer. That faith continue on earth depends *also* on us. For that reason we have to be vigilant, persevering, persistent, and continue to believe when everything turns us the other way, and even God seems to keep silence. We have to continue to pray because on that prayer depends the maintaining of faith. We must keep on praying when everything is discouraging, and when we are left with no further motive or taste for praying, because it is this prayer which causes faith to endure, which preserves it for the moment when the Son of man shall come. Such is the responsibility laid upon the constancy of prayer.

Hence prayer in its reality rests entirely on the objective existence of this commandment, an existence kept constantly alive even on the human plane by our very condition, an existence which constantly becomes "ex-sistent" (following the play on words current today). Man prays *because* God *tells* him to pray. That commandment conditions the contemporary *reality* of prayer. We encounter it in the Bible, and only there. It is by reading the Bible that man can receive this command to pray. So in a certain sense we can say that as long as Bible reading is maintained prayer is not dead, the more so since the Bible conveys not only this summons but also prayer lived historically, and ready at every moment to become our prayer.

The word of God does not transmit an external command, but one which it at the same time also carries out. Because there is the commandment to pray, there is along with it the substance of prayer. God does not issue an abstract order, but always one which is incarnate and lived in reality. That is true not only of the Psalms as the canon of Israelite prayer addressed to the God of the covenant, or of the prayers of Job in his struggle with God; we should also remember that every bearer of the word of God was a man of prayer: Abraham, Moses, David, Solomon. Each one has bequeathed us both a style of prayer, prayers which we can turn directly to our own use, and also a model of the relationship with God, which is unique and yet available to each person. To read the Bible is to read prayers, to busy oneself with prayers, and by that very fact to make progress in obedience to the commandment conveyed to us by the same text.

In that reading it is not necessary to enter into a complicated hermeneutic, into a demythologizing, for as a book of prayer the Bible is directly comprehensible and "existential." If for all the other passages, be they ethical, or theological, or historical, there is need for interpretation or retranslation, that serves no purpose as far as prayer is concerned, for the latter finds its clarification and truth in the situation in which the reader and the biblical character both find themselves. No great science is required in order to know the meaning of the prayers of a person who is suffering, who is in danger, who is set free, who is hungry, who enjoys the beauty of the world, who wants to save others. Thus the Bible *as a book of prayers* escapes the current arguments and difficulties.

OBEDIENCE

The commandment as the foundation for the reality of prayer brings us to the only discernible subjective and human motivation, namely, obedience. The only current reason for praying is acceptance of obedience to the commandment. We should well calculate, consequently, that when everything turns us away from prayer, and my heart and mind are not disposed toward it, the commandment subsists as something outside me, yet which I know is addressed to me. I know that the summons always rings out for me. So when prayer seems impossible that is no reason for panic or despair, for making a great effort, for attempting devices or techniques, for awaiting some mysterious and sovereign urge. It is enough to fall back on the most simple and child-like obedience asked of us, that of hearing the word.*

But then we must be careful. Our intellect, always defective in the things of the Spirit, will trick us into thinking that if there is obedience then there must be an obligation, a compulsion, a *duty* to pray. Then we fall back into the confusion between law and commandment. Obedience in Christ is the opposite to a duty or an obligation. There is no compulsion. There is the hearing of a word which I receive and which commands me, before which it is mine to obey without pressure or penalty. There is not a duty of prayer. There is an understanding of a responsibility, an entering into communion and dialogue.

The idea that there could be a duty (moral and objective) can lead to the supposition that obedience necessarily sterilizes prayer, which is characterized by spontaneity and involvement in a dialogue. It cannot be doubted that to declare it a duty to pray kills the possibility of prayer, that duty is impersonal and sterilizing (and not in this domain alone!). It diverts the word and command of God into a moral perspective in which God has not placed them. We well know what happened to the family prayers in the

* "The immediate person thinks and imagines that when he prays, the important thing, the thing he must concentrate upon, is that *God should hear* what HE *is praying for.* And yet in the true, eternal sense it is just the reverse: the true relation in prayer is not when God hears what is prayed for, but when *the person praying* continues to pray until he is *the one who hears,* who hears what God wills. The immediate person, therefore, uses many words and, therefore, makes demands in his prayer; the true man of prayer only *attends*" (*The Journals of Søren Kierkegaard,* trans. by Alexander Dru [New York: Oxford University Press, 1959]), p. 97. Used by permission.

old Protestant families, at which the children were obliged to be present. From the very outset that compulsion frustrated participation in the prayer. The latter can only be free and voluntary.

But that indeed is the quality of obedience in the presence of *God's* commandment. Any human commandment whatsoever claims to be strictly obligatory. An officer who issues a command leaves no avenue of escape whereby obedience might be avoided. But precisely the commandment of God is another matter altogether, for it is always the God of Jesus Christ who gives it, even when he is the God of Sinai or of Sodom: the God of Jesus Christ, that is to say the God who is incarnate in the human condition, who empties himself, who dies, because he loves man. He was that when he created the worlds, for from the very beginning he had left his creation free not to love him. Hence this commandment, since it is of God, calls us to a free obedience, to a voluntary consent, to a response that one cannot hesitate to call spontaneous, even though incited. There is no question of a duty or of threats.

Merely to feel summoned, to feel invited, like the friends in the parable of the feast, with the possibility always open of refusing the invitation (which certainly was a commandment), yet knowing also that this commandment offers something which previously we had thought impossible—this simply attests the fact that all that had seemed to me infinitely difficult, a crushing responsibility, without content, is now within my reach, on my own intellectual level, part of the available assets (real, even though rationally I neither feel nor see the reality) of my life. Thus obedience to this commandment does not falsify prayer. It is a sufficient reason for praying and for praying in truth. It does not frustrate the experience of prayer, a reality which infinitely transcends the reason.

Of course, once prayer is born it has no further need for reasons, but the problem we are wrestling with is that of its birth. This obedience which leaves us so free, so completely ourselves, possesses nevertheless a great efficacy (not of itself, surely, but because it is an obedience to *this* commandment *of God,* who is himself efficacious). This obedience, in fact, transforms my condition, in the sense that everything in my life which was an obstacle to prayer— impossibilities, lukewarmness, all the causes, justifications, conditions, dispositions and situations, inward as well as outward, which keep me from praying—is called into question.

Listening to the commandment, and the decision to obey it, by no means imply passivity, but direct combat against the whole context in which my inability to pray was located. Obedience is in no sense a submissive, passive, insipid, feeble attitude. Obedience is an active struggle with all that impedes the reality of life in Christ; hence, in this connection, with every obstacle to prayer.*

* This foundation based on obedience to the commandment seems to me more true, more biblical, more sound, than Bonhoeffer's statement on the discipline of the arcane. The return to a certain esoterism of revelation does not appear to me to conform either to the proclamation of salvation or to the trend of revelation. Prayer cannot be based on a secret knowledge. But certainly as an obedience it implies a discipline of the hidden, of the secret, a discipline of prayer which each one is called upon to apply to himself, for quite obviously even a spontaneous prayer, even a prayer connected with an event, cannot simply be an improvised outburst. Because it is obedience it is intentional, thoughtful, disciplined.

In speaking of struggle we do not have in mind a discursive intellectual struggle, nor a theoretical critique. Lived obedience *is,* in itself, this calling into question of all disobedience. Christians ought to admit that if, on the one hand, it is right to accept all questioning by people in general, by society, by science, by history, by politics and economics, on the other hand, when it comes to our understanding of revelation they have the vocation of faith and of life to make the questioning reciprocal. Every act and decision of the Christian life contests that which the world sets up in opposition in terms of conditions and reasons for not leading that Christian life.

Psychology (pseudo-psychology?) and sociology (pseudo-sociology?) claim to demonstrate that prayer is a "religious rescue," a magic practice, an escape from the serious, a "superstitious vanity" (Kant), a means of shuffling off one's human responsibilities, one element in the over-all strategy of desire (Freud), a religious alienation (Feuerbach), a withdrawal (Robinson). Then theology joins the chorus and accepts all these charges without more ado. It is true that they put us on our guard against false prayer, but they also destroy from within the person who prays.

However, instead of its being these analyses and the various theologies based on them, which judge prayer, the fact is that in the presence of the commandment to pray and to watch, we must completely reverse the position. Far from its being these sciences and theologies which judge prayer, it is the commandment which constrains us to judge the theologies, for this commandment is independent of scientific analyses.

The person who takes on vigilance is no longer an object of those observations, for he depends upon another order, and we find that the theologies which conform to the scientific imperatives, whatever be their claims, are really theologies of slumber and not of vigilance, of conformity and uncertainty, under the guise of pseudo-lucidity, of honesty, of a summons. They satisfy man by intransigence and scientific apparatus, and justify him in not believing, or praying, or watching. The absolute nature of their seeming exactitude is the expression of the dark desire to conform to the milieu and not to be left alone responsible, and as watchmen in a spiritual night, which science teaches us not to believe in, in order to have us take our place in a hermeneutic labyrinth.

But if the commandment to pray is to become the reason for praying, that is to say, is to lead us to obedience, we need obviously to take it with radical seriousness. We need to receive it as a radical commandment. That is possible only if we receive it in faith. The word read in the Bible is not a commandment for me unless it enters through the door of faith. Thus prayer presupposes faith. It is then that obedience comes alive. To raise the problem of prayer, of the difficulty of praying, etc., is in reality to raise the problem of faith in the contemporary world.

Yet we must not say that for prayer to take place and to arise spontaneously "it suffices to have faith." Let us recall once more that we never *have* faith, but as far as we are concerned we must recognize especially that in our day a dissociation tends to enter in. Earnest Christians trying to live the faith come to the point of giving up prayer. That is when the commandment and obedience are indispensable, and when obedience is indeed the reason for prayer.

But the word read in the Bible cannot be heard as a personal commandment except by faith. The recognition that that word comes from a person who is summoning me is a recognition of faith. The acceptance of the passage in which I read the commandment as susceptible of being the word of God is an act of faith. The decision of obedience to this commandment is a decision of faith. How often the Epistles remind us that the first expression of faith is prayer, *"First of all,* then, I urge that supplications, prayers, intercessions, and thanksgivings be made for all men," says Paul (I Timothy 2:1). Prayer comes before all the rest in the life in Christ. It is the concrete expression, the touchstone, of faith. All the rest of the life in Christ flows from prayer. The whole ethic and behavior of Christians rests on the practice of prayer, but this practice is that of faith *alone.*

Consequently, every other root which is sought for prayer is sterile and without purpose. It is not a question of natural prayer, of spontaneous sentiment, of spiritual elevation, of the prayer of pagans, of unbelievers. We know that all that exists, but we cannot graft what the God of Jesus Christ expects as prayer, what Jesus Christ commands us to pray, on that. The one phenomenon is not a continuation of the other. All the reasons for not praying are addressed to the first, but are contested, as we have said, by the second. If we feel these obstacles as affecting our prayer to Jesus Christ and to the Father, that means that we are living in confusion concerning what that prayer is in truth.

Surely one can ask oneself, "What meaning does prayer have in the environment of our society, in the midst of secularization, or irreligion? What meaning does prayer have for the man of *this* modern society?" But I think that is a false question, for in any event and in all epochs prayer can only be an expression of faith. Hence there is no reason to be concerned with prayer in relation to the indifferent person in our society. The problem of prayer is not his. He is outside it and he can only begin to be concerned through a recognition that Jesus is the Christ, that is, through his conversion, to use an outmoded term. Yet we have to recognize that to a certain extent prayer does concern him as well, for it is just this unchurched person, this grown-up person, this secularized person, who prays all the false prayers with which our age abounds! Nothing will turn him aside from his implicit faiths. It is all a matter of knowing what faith and to whom it is addressed.

Likewise, the content of Christian prayer, of which Scripture furnishes so many examples, can only be the speech of faith, and prayer is itself a decision of faith. Just as faith is an act of my responsibility before God, so prayer is a decision of my responsibility of faith. "It is *in* human willing that the will of God operates," says Ott. But this rigorous connection between faith and prayer should make us aware of the converse. If, for the Christian, prayer becomes impossible, dead, troublesome, uncertain, that does not spring in the first instance from all the causes we have enumerated. The sole basic problem is that we do not make the decision to obey, since we do not take the commandment seriously, and if that is the case it is because we are not living the faith which has its foundation in Jesus Christ.

It is this lack of faith which is here in question. The absence of prayer and the difficulty of praying are the evidence for the absence of faith. We know very well that faith is never a purely individual act. It is always based on the faith held in common by the people of God, and the personal difficulty in praying corresponds to the lack of meaning in ritual, canonical, and collective prayers, just as the absence of personal faith corresponds to the crisis of faith in the Church. We cannot expect to restore personal prayer by shifting it in the direction of the prayer of public worship, nor can we revive the latter by injecting personal ardor into it. The two go together. How can we pretend that prayer is *primarily* communal, when to the contrary we see Jesus seeking to be alone and to withdraw from the crowd, even from his own disciples, in order to pray. He always retired alone (that is why we have so few "prayers of Jesus" in the Gospels). Never do the Gospel writers present him as praying *with* them. Yet this secret, solitary, individual prayer is never enclosed within the self. Moses, face to face with God, carried all the people with him.

Thus faith in the God of Jesus Christ implies that I take the commandment seriously, consequently that it commands *me* to pray; but much more—since that is the case I can say that no faith is possible without prayer. To pretend that faith is expressed in witnessing, in service, in involvement, in self-abnegation, or in preaching, is all quite true, but without prayer, in the neglect of prayer, it all becomes false. Prayer is not a work of faith. It is the possibility of the work of faith. That is why we are told to pray *without ceasing,* for faith is completely sterile without this respiration.

That is one of the problems of the "new theologies." In

consequence of the desire to make the message (kerygma) valid for all, to see all men as in the presence of God, to increase the universality of the lordship of Jesus Christ, to insist on the value of mankind generally (to the detriment of the Christian), to insist on the value of the world (to the detriment of the Church), one comes to the point of denying whatever can only be specifically Christian. The first victim of these trends of thought is prayer, and it must not be supposed that the depreciation is without its effect. It has its repercussions on the faith itself, which can no longer subsist or manifest itself under these conditions.

The crisis of prayer makes us face up to the difficulty of the faith which the "new theologies" are taking into account (the theologies of the death of God, of revolution, of interpretation, of demythologizing, etc.). If we cannot pray, that is ultimately because we do not believe that God acts, that he is a creator, that he takes a hand in reality (we now prefer to see him included within reality, ultimately subject to the same hazards as we). From another point of view we do not believe that God would want to change his will to suit our prayer, to lead us to where his will and ours would be in agreement.

Prayer is a mirror in which we are called to contemplate our spiritual state. Since it is a real encounter with God we can in prayer see ourselves as God sees us. Since it is a real encounter with God, the lack of prayer forces us to consider the lack of reality in our faith, which should not cause us to retreat further into that negation, to shut ourselves up in the hard fact of the absence of faith, and subsequently to deny the possibility of praying. We should, rather, in the end take to ourselves that attitude which becomes the open door to all prayer and the prologue to all contemporary prayer: "I believe, help my unbelief."

The Assertion of Freedom

Prayer as obedience is an act of freedom. In every situation other than the encounter with the commandment of God it is dependent, subject to all the causes and circumstances of which we have spoken, which is to say that then it is an expression of a prior cultural fact, of an education, of a sensibility, etc. We have seen that all the human reasons for praying have disappeared from our Western society. Wherefore prayer depends on my decision to pray, on the choice which I make in that direction. Hence, to obey the commandment is an act of freedom relative to the environmental circumstances, since in this case I am going counter to these determining factors. So now to find myself in the situation we have described incites me to make a free decision. Therefore we should not bemoan the disappearance of the human reasons for prayer.*

---

* It might here be supposed that I am adopting the same attitude as that which I was criticizing above in connection with faith, according to which the loss of the human substratum, of every reason for believing in the God of Jesus Christ is splendid because it means that faith is now purified, having become a totally independent decision of the person. In reality, however, what I am here saying with regard to prayer is quite different, for I am assuming another attitude both toward God and toward man; toward God to the extent to which everything depends on obedience (and not on a critique of what is addressed to me as the word of God), toward man to the extent to which prayer is a crucial factor. Nowhere am I suggesting a justification of the present social situation or of the human being it produces.

But if I am free in my decision to pray, that is not an automatic freedom, resulting from social evolution. It is a consequence of the intervention of the word of God, which is always liberating in and of itself. When the summons of the commandment reaches me, it liberates me at the same time in order to make my response a free response. My prayer can only be a form of freedom, without which it is nothing. But freedom is not a quality or a characteristic of my being. I am freed by prayer, and I live freedom fully in prayer. It is when Moses obeys the command to go up on Mount Sinai that he receives the most amazing freedom which man could ever have, that of speaking with God as friend with friend. It is when we obey the commandment of Jesus that we discover the reality of God as Father, and that we have the unapproachable freedom of saying, "Our Father."

To call him Father is to open two paths of freedom, stemming from this freedom which God grants me so to name him. It bears witness, first of all, to the fact that I cannot be free except through the gift of liberation, that is to say, my liberty will only be true through the mediation of the heteronomy of the one to whom I am appealing. This is to say that the prayer to the Father affirms the fact that my freedom, my coming of age as a man, is of a piece with my sonship. J. A. T. Robinson (with whom I agree, for once) has expressed it very well. In essence he says: Man having come of age is still called to be a son. Sonship in the New Testament is an image of freedom, and is used precisely to describe the man who has passed his minority and has reached his majority. The Christian faith, far from seeking to keep man in chains, calls him to maturity, not that of the adolescent rebelling *against* a father, but that of an adult who enters into the responsible liberty of a son and heir.

Then we also have the other aspect of this freedom. In praying to the Father I escape from the ambiguity, the muddle, the confusion in which I find myself in attempting to distinguish intellectually between the true Father and the false "father" who is the object of my desire. Prayer is an avowal that I shall never succeed by myself in purifying and authenticating my faith, in discerning theologically who is God. It gives me the freedom from having to rack my brains in an attempt to escape the Freudian father who is a product of my fancy. It is the invocation of God against my gods, of the true Father against the subconscious images of my will, and that suffices. In and through that invocation, I am free indeed.

It takes foolishness and an unbelievable vanity to analyze the gift which Jesus gives us of calling God "Father" in terms of paternalism and an anthropocentrism which is culturally outmoded. That God invites us to call him Father, that he summons us to assume *that* liberty, how can that be denatured under the guise of demythologizing, to the point of making him say the opposite to what was said? What weight does our claim to autonomy and maturity have in the presence of that liberty? What can it mean to declare oneself independent of that God? It can only mean to submit to the conditioning, the enslavement, the demands and the limitations of our sociological milieu, our politics, our rationality, our passions, and our pretensions. But what freedom do we know in all that? To be sure, subjected by our so-called critical scientific spirit to the conditions of our culture, we can relativize the word of God. We can deal with it through successive reductions, in consequence of which it ceases to be liberating for us and we lose the ability to pray.

Hence, we have a choice to make. We have to decide, knowing that the wonderful way (that of hermeneutics, for example) which man opens up for himself deprives him both of prayer and of freedom. It is the narrow way intellectually, but the broad way of slavery and of death spiritually.

Now the decision I should make in full knowledge is the decision to pray to this Lord who is the Father. But that decision, taken on my own responsibility, responds to a word which indeed has already been addressed to me. It is because of this prior word that prayer is a dialogue with God. I am not here referring to the word of the commandment, but to that which was addressed to each one of us in Jesus Christ from the beginning of the world, that which is aimed at us and which we at the same time await, that which is creative of us and in us, that which manifests the being and at the same time the purpose of God, as God has revealed them.

Prayer, however fervent, spontaneous and new, is never other than a sequel, a consequence, a response, to the word of invitation first made known in Scripture. It is discerned as word through faith and is received as the word of God by the action of God alone. It is futile to believe in an authentication on our own, or in a transformation of Scripture into word by means of a method. If it is not God who is speaking, then there is nothing.

But that corresponds to the experience of the person who

prays. Even if he has the feeling that his prayer is vanishing into the void and is leading only to resignation, nevertheless it still remains a dialogue, and he knows it. Even if God is felt to be "mute, blind and deaf to the cry of his creatures," still the person who prays is never engaging in a monologue. The prayer always reverts to that of Elijah in the wilderness: "It is enough; now, O Lord, take away my life." I have done what I thought right. I am defeated. All is lost. It is all over. That prayer in the darkness is always taken up by that of Jesus: "My God, my God, why hast thou forsaken me?" It is to the empty heavens that he appeals, in the forsakenness which he experiences as total. Yet he still says, "My God." This God *is*. He is *mine*. Even with that much said, all can still in fact be lost. But the relationship is established, even in this absence.

Thus we often have the impression that this is a monologue, and that basically it is we who are summoning God. But in the deepest part of ourselves we know that it is indeed a dialogue, and that we would not be opening our mouths if we did not sense that fact. The relationship is begun before the idea of praying occurs to us. The summons which reaches us and the commandment which concerns us are nothing other than the order to continue the dialogue. When my emotions, the tragedy or the joy of the situation, push me to take the initiative and to turn fervently to a God who may not be there, and who is certainly silent, lo, I enter upon an open dialogue established from the very beginning, whether I do so knowingly (having read the Scriptures), or unknowingly (having been cut off from them).

God seeks that relationship of prayer, whether he interrogates (Adam, where are you? Cain, what have you done to

your brother?) or whether he proclaims (Behold I will . . .),
whether he gives or whether he takes away (Job), whether
he commands or whether he receives in mercy (Jonah); in
all instances he looks for a response on the part of the man
who prays, and who in this way enters into the dialogue.
This dialogue is an expression of the "history together"
which God, Emanuel, wills to have with mankind. He cannot tolerate the lonely word from either side. He has never
acquiesced in the break which was brought about in Adam.

But we need to be fully aware of the fact that this relationship does not take place on the level of service, whether
cultural or social, nor on the level of morality, nor on that of
a dissertation, nor on that of the community life. All is rooted
in this privileged, unique, essential dialogue of prayer, in
which, in the final analysis, I never have the initiative. Otherwise, prayer would in fact be a discourse, a monologue, and
we have lived it and have known that such is not the case.

If engaging in this dialogue is a possibility, if the carrying
out of the commandment means something other than the
application of a law, if obedience implies freedom, that is
because the commandment involves something other than
an imperative. "Watch and pray," and certain texts add,
"that ye may . . ."—that must not be understood as point-
ing to an objective to be achieved, or a recompense which
might possibly be granted us. The "that ye may" is not what
should motivate the prayer, nor should it convert it into a
link in the chain of human causality. What is understood in
the commandment is a promise, which has a number of
facets.

It is a promise, first of all, that prayer is really possible.

When God says, "Call upon me," he is saying by that: What you shall say is truly prayer, truly speech, a speech which really reaches me and is really a participation in a dialogue with me. However unthinkable, incomprehensible (in the strict sense), inscrutable, also useless in our estimation, impossible of realization, prayer may be, nevertheless it genuinely takes place. That is because God guarantees the establishment of the communication, though we cannot be certain of it except by paying attention to the command. The latter contains the promise that God, in issuing *that* order (and not some arbitrary decree of a mad potentate), gives at the same time to obedient prayer the import, the weight, the substance, and the clarity which keep it from being lost in the void, in the absence, in the nothingness. It takes its place in a prior relationship, that of the incarnation of God in Jesus.

But the promise is also one of answers to prayer. Surely this is not a mere matter of automation. We shall be dealing with that again later on. Yet our certainty of prayer rests upon the assurance that, once heard and received, it will be answered. Ask and it shall be given you. There can be no doubt about it. What is here being declared is the whole attitude of the God of Jesus Christ. He cannot fail to give to him who asks. That promise is contained and made rigorously binding in the commandment itself. If we accept the one we must at the same time accept the other. If we believe in the one we must also (sometimes in spite of the evidence) believe in the other, and if our faith causes us to obey the commandment, we have also to know that it is part of the obedience of faith to be assured that God responds.

To be sure, it has frequently been observed that this response does not necessarily bring about the precise answer we were asking for, nor does it imply the exact solutions which we had in mind. There can be another outcome, and the one which God chooses is more true, even if disconcerting to us. The moment of the response is the best possible even if we seem to have waited interminably between the prayer and its answer.

Finally, also, even the absence of an answer is a solution when God by his silence forces me to wrestle with the question, or the obstacle, myself. The absence of an answer is for me the obligation received from God to resolve for myself the problem which I took to God. But then what value does prayer have if ultimately I have to manage by myself, if the miracle failed to take place?

This is the weak understanding of our egocentric minds, of our ability to be amazed without being able to observe. Launch out into the deep and you shall see. What happens then is that the strength is not your strength, but that of the word which is spoken to you (and which always awaits you). "Go with the strength that you have." You are not left to your own abilities. Your prayer is answered, not because the situation is miraculously cleared up, but because you have been granted exactly as much strength and ability (which previously you did not have of yourself) as is necessary to surmount the difficulty and resolve the problem. Moreover, you do not know it. You do not see it (for even in prayer we always have eyes for seeing nothing), but the passage which you have to read has become readable. The situation is inwardly and secretly changed, yet not so as to make it possible for you to see it except for the purpose of setting out to attack the difficulty. Launch out into the deep and cast your net. You do not know it, but the fish are there waiting for you, even though all through the night they were not there. Launch out.

There were also the Levites bearing the Ark on their shoulders. They were obliged to advance into the Jordan, and they did not know at first that the Jordan would recede before them. They had to enter the water up to their shoulders before God's work became manifest.

Yet, with our incredulity toward prayer, we expect the fish to jump by themselves into the boat (and we will merely row ashore once the miracle is performed). We expect a clear, well-marked road (it would be better if it were asphalted, and still better if we had a map) to open up before us as far as the eye can see. We must be assured that the Jordan, for its part, is going to obey God. We are indeed ready to go ahead after the miracle has been wrought.

I say that that is the prayer of incredulity, that it is not a prayer at all. If I expect an answer of that kind, then what I speak is not a prayer, and consequently there will be no answer. My strength will not be increased. The situation will not be mysteriously changed.

The promise of an answer (and if I take prayer seriously, how can I fail to receive this promise with assurance?) implies on my part the risk of becoming involved in the action of the prayer. There is no prayer without risk. Prayer is never made in order to escape the risk of faith, or to be dispensed from doing what God gives us to do. The moment a prayer is received by God, his answer is to give us to do what he considers good, with all the means for doing it. Prayer is a dialogue, but *this* particular dialogue. God acts and requires us to act. In the prayer, and the promise which is attached to it, we must work along with him. Then prayer is fully answered.

Finally, the commandment is a promise in that we know that God brings these prayers together to unite them into a whole, the prayer of all the saints. Since there is this promise, therefore I can also know that the encounter lived in prayer can be genuine. We must get away from the idea that prayer is contained in the encounter with the other person. So many encounters take place which bring me to the despair of an impossible dialogue. Rather, it is the encounter comprised within prayer which gives me genuine access to the other person, because of this promise of the gathering together. I can then refer to the Father the missed encounter, the dialogue of misunderstandings, in order to render them possible once again. I can lean on the promise, so that my prayer might let me penetrate the sin which separates us from one another.

The commandment is the promise that our most lonely, most private, most personal prayer is gathered in, is recapitulated by the Lord, together with that of the whole Church, of all generations, of all the solitary individuals, and of all the communities. The communion of saints need not necessarily be affirmed as a concrete and visible reality. It is already contained in the simple commandment to pray, addressed to all the saints. It is realized in the prayer of each one of them. Certainly we know that the prayer which Jesus has taught us is a prayer of all, even though said by each one —*Our* Father . . . , *our* bread. . . . It is a glorious promise that the moment I say "our" I am joined with all those who have said it, with Jesus first of all. I am joined, bound, integrated, and assimilated. The command implies that order, that putting in order of the true Church and of love.

How, in such circumstances, can prayer be the passive and dismal carrying out of a constraint? If it is received with its rich promise, then the commandment, as a sufficient foundation for my prayer, is fully satisfying to my spiritual life. Therefore, prayer is no longer oriented toward a conditioning, determining past, of which I feel the terrible sociological weight, the cumulative effect of which I know very well I am unable to overcome. Is one to pray, still carrying the weight of the past? Is he to pray, saying at the outset, "It is impossible, nothing has changed in the past, why should it change in the future? I have continued to sin in spite of so many prayers, so will I not be a hypocrite, continuing to pray under those conditions, when I know in advance that I will not be transformed? The war has gone on in spite of my prayers. Why will it stop tomorrow?" To pray with those thoughts in one's heart (and I know very well that they are there necessarily, dear Reader, if you are concerned, as I am) is still to pray for all the futile motives which come and go, an emotion, an agony, a spiritual feeling. It is not to pray for the only essential reason, obedience to the commandment.

If you simply take that commandment and face up to it, then all the scruples are done away with. Also, you know then that the crushing past which paralyzes prayer with its demon, that implacable past which appears to you to be the absolute cause of your situation (and which kills you by the very fact that it looks like the cause of your prayer), that past no longer exists for you. If you take seriously the commandment to pray, or, rather, him who says it to you, then you know that your past is taken up by him. Henceforth it no longer belongs to you, nor you to it. He to whom you speak and who spoke first to you has taken charge of it. He now has it in hand. You are now a man without a past, without ties, without roots, without conditioning in the dialogue of prayer. You are at that instant a new man and the sequence of your life takes place on another stage, at another level. But that is true only in prayer, and on condition of truly obeying the commandment.

One is not a new man in order to live this tête-à-tête unbrokenly and to bring about this ceaselessly renewed novelty. The disciples on Mount Tabor wanted to remain there, to contemplate endlessly the triumphal vision and the gathering of the witnesses of the past. But it was necessary to come down, to throw themselves into that future which was to be so much more decisive than the moment of transfiguration and without which the latter would have no meaning. They were projected into the future by reason of the promise contained in the commandment.

Prayer (and otherwise what would it be?) is the begetting of a future. It is not there to complete a past, nor to assure a present. It is there to realize a future, to assure the possibility of a history, the history of my own life, that it be not the gloomy repetition of undefined moments without meaning. It is there to assure the history of my church, that it be not the inconsistency of good intentions and of formless pieties. It is there to assure the history of my people, that it be not an accumulation of oppressions, of hatreds and injustices. That is to say that prayer is there in order that there might truly be a history at all levels, and not a succession of futile, meaningless actions.

Now let us not be deceived. It is prayer, and prayer alone, which can make history. We shall come back to that. To pray is to carry oneself toward the future. It is both to expect it as possible, and to will it as history, but the one possible of God and the history of God with man. What would prayer be if it did not claim to make present, at this moment and in whatever concerns us, this meeting of God with man brought to pass in Jesus Christ? Therefore, it has the effect of affirming that henceforth this is our way of life, that the history to be made is not economic, not political, not esthetic, not social, but in all these spheres it is the history of God with man. The decision to produce this history was made in Jesus Christ. Prayer, my prayer now, is the decision of man to produce it also and at the same time. Prayer is that or nothing.

Thus prayer, because based on the promise contained in the commandment, implies hope. It is an act and an expression of hope, even if (especially if) on the human level it is a cry of despair. That is the point at which we link up with experience. As a true prayer it is also a true experience, not the experience of prior successes, nor of blessed states of soul. If it were the latter, how would we avoid subjectivism and changing moods? As a mere experience my prayer can depend on a good or a poor digestion. A magnificent view of the ocean puts the praise of God in my soul, just as the fear of an accident makes me turn to God for help.

But what happens apart from these circumstances? How are we to avoid the tie with the past? If I knew in the past the value of prayer, that tie accrues to me from a past of prayer. If I carry out the dialogue of which prayer consists, that is because I interpreted it through the medium of a hundred past dialogues.

Yet the fact is that prayer is in no way a satisfaction, or a centering on the self, or an attachment to the past. Let us recapitulate what we had already noted: prayer as the expression of hope when I am in despair, as a dialogue of faith when I am in doubt. It comes in to contradict the actual, concrete situation in which I am. It is the experience of that contradiction. The dialogue with God sets me up in conflict with myself, with my milieu, with my past. Since it is a dialogue, how can it be otherwise?

Furthermore, is there dialogue if the two parties are in such agreement that there is nothing to say? A dialogue implies reserve, tension, contradiction, argument back and forth. What meaning does prayer have if it is a way of saying to God, "I am a wonderful person, because you have made me wonderful"? What is there left here for God to say? Complete agreement means silence. Also, we have made the acquaintance of that prayer elsewhere. It was that of the Pharisee in the temple, and when Jesus says that the Pharisee returned to his house without being justified, he is saying that his prayer did not share in the dialogue with God, but in the silence of God.

Prayer is a protest against myself, such is one attempt

at prayer which I can make, but when I have done that I can be sure that the prayer does not come from the bottom of my heart. How can I know this? Does it not often come about that people criticize themselves? Is not the situation in which God has nothing to say a simple matter of seeing things clearly? If we continue along that line, all we shall show is that we have not yet understood anything about prayer, for man's self-criticism is always negative. It is a clash between clearsightedness and one's inborn, natural good conscience, whereas the contradiction of prayer is the reverse of that. It is, rather, the challenge which hope offers to my despair. It is the impugning of my anguish, of my pessimism, through joy. It is the bursting of my bonds through freedom. It does all that without giving me even the shadow of a good conscience, for in prayer I know very well (and through direct experience with that without which there is no prayer) that this joy, this freedom, and this hope do not come from me.

Such is the genuine experience I want to live of the dialogue of prayer which is opened up to me. I can live it, but I cannot make use of it. I cannot save some of it over for tomorrow, nor can I set up an uninterrupted purring of faith and prayer on a base of undisturbed convictions. This experience is lightninglike, and it cannot be retained. Tomorrow, I am simply called to begin the dialogue all over again, since the commandment and the hope are addressed to me endlessly.

Tomorrow, "Watch and pray." These are two actions indissolubly united. Prayer is an act of vigilance and the vigilance is a consequence of prayer (not a prior condition). If you pray, you can be watchful. It will be possible for you to watch with me. But the disciples were not praying. They were not doing anything during Gethsemane. They were waiting. Then they fell asleep. Prayer would have made them watchful, and that brings us to the answer to prayer.

Apart from its particular intention, prayer produces watchfulness within us. That is an answer, the third form of the answer. We are not vigilant, attentive, clearsighted, and watchful as a result of our intellects and our wills, but because these things are bestowed upon us as a response to our prayer, which is itself an act of watchers. We are kept awake by the dialogue itself. The act of relating to God obviously prevents our falling asleep, just as vigilance guarantees to prayer its substance. How can we say anything serious, authentic, or committed before God, if we are dozing dreamers, awakened out of sleep, complacent and satisfied, if we are looking always at ourselves, contemplating our persons in our glory or in our dissatisfactions, in our pride or in our sin, if we live in a daze, if we evolve in a world which is idealistic in its concepts and ideas?

Vigilance presupposes observation and expectation, hope and clearsightedness, spiritual discernment and concrete realism, perseverance and availability. Vigilance nourishes prayer with its clear view of what needs to be done in this world, of what needs to be petitioned for the people of this society. That leads to a prayer which is both to the point and substantial, not a vague, formless stammering. At the same time, vigilance nourishes prayer with a discernment of the works of God in this age, within these people and in these events, works of God stemming from and contained within the great work of God. "Watch with me"—there is no vigilance without that relationship to Jesus Christ, to the constantly renewed vigilance of Jesus Christ, leading to a prayer which is joyful, full of power and hope, even if it be that of Gethsemane.

But the discernment of the works of God is not possible without a clear view of the tragic events of the world. The gold-panner has to stir tons of sand in his pan before uncovering a little gold dust, and no realism concerning the *actual* reality of the world is possible except from the standpoint of the promises of God.* The gold-panner would not stir those tons of sand if he were not aware of the presence of the gold.

Thus vigilance looks two ways. It looks toward the events of the world in which prayer finds its material. Surely that involves attention not only to particular situations but to general factors as well, which are "political" in the etymological sense of the word, everything, that is, which affects man in our society. So vigilance applies *also* to the political situation, but it cannot be a genuine vigilance, it cannot bring forth a true prayer, unless it is first of all (and at the same time) the vigilance of the return. That is when prayer receives its full import, the import of eschatological prayer, which means a prayer of combat. It is prayer today because centered on that coming event, on the End of the Age in the glory of the presence of the Lord.

Thus prayer, which seems to us to be based on a past act, the commandment which has been given, receives in

* J. Ellul, "Sur le Réalism chrétien," in *Foi et Vie* (1956).

reality its significance from the already present coming of the Son of man, and if that is so it is because the commandment itself orients us toward that coming. The word, two millenniums old, heard as coming from the past, obliges us to look ahead. Watch and pray that the Son of man may find you standing and watching. Prayer, obedient to the commandment and based on nothing else, continued by persons who transmit the command of the Lord from generation to generation, is then like a thread stretched between the past and the future, binding the ages together in a contemporary unity, and the concert of people in the unity of the Church.

5 ❁

PRAYER AS COMBAT

That prayer is a combat has been said hundreds of times,* but that (as well as the aspect of dialogue) means that there is no oneness. If there were oneness between God and the world, there would be no prayer. The relationship of prayer is already evidence of the lack of that oneness, which is confirmed by the fact that prayer is a combat. We are not looking for the enduring nature of prayer, nor for its theological def-

---

* "Believe me, I think there is nothing which requires more effort than to pray to God. . . . Prayer demands combat to the last breath," says a desert Father (*Apophthegms of the Fathers,* P.G. 65, 112 B).

"True prayer is a struggle with God, in which one triumphs through the triumph of God" (Kierkegaard, *Journals,* I; trans. C.E.H.).

inition. We are asking simply whether prayer can be anything other than a combat in this day and age, and what the specific characteristics of the combat of prayer are in our world.

In an Age of Abandonment

Perhaps we are living in an age in which God "turns away his face," an age of abandonment. Such an age is described in the Gospel apocalypses as that moment "between the times" in which man no longer discerns any truth, in which power runs rampant, in which there is constant confusion between evil and good (you will call good evil, and evil good), in which man gives rein to every presumption and experiences every terror, in which anguish increases to the point where it is fatal of itself to those who come within its grasp. It is a time of frenzied persecutions, when the very best fall to the sword. This is an age in which, in our shortsighted wisdom, we imagine that God is dead, because we had reduced to nothing our trumped-up concept of the God who escapes us. It is a time in which all kinds of messiahs make their appearance pretending to save mankind. One is called Father. Another is known as a leader of nations. A third is called Redeemer, a fourth Messenger. It is a time in which our wisdoms dissolve God's wisdom, in order to render his understanding more and more refined. It is a time in which our prayers are not answered. We cry out to heaven, and receive no reply. It is a time in which man proudly calls himself adult, only to find that he is a wretched orphan.

There is no need for the stars to fall from heaven, for the sun to flicker or the earth to tremble. What is taking place in the heart of man is already the eradication of every measure and norm. What is taking place around man is a surge of forces which are mastered and let loose at the same time, which are plunged into darkness in the name of the light on which man thought to lay his hand. It is the time of trial at the end of the age, in which man no longer feels any need to know God, in which the language of God has become dead, and in which God remains silent to those who call upon him.

If it be true that we are living in this time of abandonment (which is neither historically unique nor final), then prayer is all the more urgent and necessary. But it represents a battle to be fought on all fronts. In the first place, the combat of prayer is a combat in spite of everything. It is one of obeying the commandment (as we saw in the preceding chapter) in spite of common sense. This obedience is still demanded of us even if our prayers are not heard, even if we no longer know what prayer means. That is to say that what is expected of us is a radical trust, to the point of the absurd, since in that case prayer acquires its reality, its value, its sense, from that which we do not see.

But that is the most immediate aspect of the combat. In order to accept it one must have traveled a long road in the faith. If one is to be satisfied with the secret answers of which we have spoken, a long discipline of life is required. In that loneliness it will seem to us as though the watchfulness were *ours* alone, that of our eyes peering into the silent night. It will look to us as though the battle were being fought with our own strength, left to its own resources. What is required is a blind act of faith here and now, if one is to be aware of the contrary.

Let no one reproach me at this point for using the word "blind." It is not a theological thesis. I mean by it neither the *Credo quia absurdum,* nor that one has to become blind in order to see the truth. If I use the word "blind," it is because that *is our present situation.* We are blind through the excessive refinement of a hermeneutic which removes that which could have been seen. We are blind because in this night of abandonment no light of the intellect or the feelings is available to us. Blindness is not a superior quality of faith. We are blind, and for that reason we are not capable of any other but a blind act of faith, like the blind man, who, though he did not see Jesus, yet called him the Son of David. In this irrational decision we know the opposite of what we think we are experiencing. We see the Lord. Then prayer is exactly what Bonhoeffer defined it to be, "the break in the circle of anxious hesitations" and "the confrontation with the tempest of events." How can it fail to be a combat?

Prayer and the Self

Must we say that it is first of all a combat against the self? That already appears in everything we have written. The time of abandonment is something that we live and feel within ourselves. The Christian has found discord, doubt, and the loss of the joyful certainties, so we have to struggle on that score to conquer and convince ourselves. Each time we undertake to pray it is a victory over temptation, over the giving up of the struggle with the self, over the divided heart. Through prayer, man, in fact, avoids anguish and the divided self, but to pray is the last action he can think to take to come out of his own tragedy and destruction.

Whereas the situation in the world leads to the break-up of man into a series of irreconcilable patterns, and to the splintering of the personality through scattered activities, prayer, on the other hand, reunifies. But this reunification does not go without saying. It involves the discovery of God here below, in this very abandonment. It is a will, an energy of obedience. Prayer, then, escapes two falsehoods, that of giving up and that of unlimited conflict. But in order to receive this oneness, a person has to will to go against that which is most natural and most obvious in and around himself.

We were speaking of that "distraction" which causes us not to pray because of our being scattered in all directions. Now we find that, even before receiving oneness in prayer, we must get ourselves together in order to want to pray; "get ourselves together," that is, as one speaks of a horse gathering his forces when he is about to put out a great effort to jump over a crucial hurdle. We must take in hand all the scattered parts of the self, all those energies applied to this or that task, all the attentions and affections, all the strengths and despairs, all the understandings and humiliations. If this totality is not brought together, then we cannot pray, seduced and distracted as we are by a hundred sights which are more attractive and more obvious than prayer. To pray goes against the natural bent that I instinctively am because inclined that way by my culture, my surroundings, and my work. There is already a combat here, at the most humble level.

In addition, we shall have to conquer ourselves in the face of that gnawing doubt, the continual question, "What's the use?" It is not merely a matter of wanting to pray, but of praying a *genuine* prayer. On that score we are caught up in a struggle against the life-direction given by our consumer society, which neither knows nor is able to suggest as the meaning of our work, the joy of our life, and the value of our society anything other than a higher level of consumption.

Prayer, introduced into this practice and ideology, is itself swept along by the current and takes its bearings in relation to consumption. It makes no sense to a person such as I am unless it paves the way for an increase in consumer goods. At its most rudimentary level, the prayer of petition has for its purpose to assure us of goods which are useful, and surely superfluous, which are determined by what we today find to be essential. That which seems to be due us in a society such as ours we petition God for (if we get as far as to pray). Since we consider ourselves the victims of injustice, we are frustrated when we do not have the bizarre possessions set before us by industry. God becomes the agent for satisfying the needs created by our society.

If we manage to avoid that trap, through respect for God's majesty and the act of self-emptying whereby he gives himself to us, we still are not safe from the passion to consume, for our prayer can be an effort at spiritual consumption, the consumption of God. Each one of us is so profoundly patterned in accordance with this necessity to consume that everything we lay hold of we value from that standpoint, even God. Furthermore, prayer is only a phase of the various enterprises of man, with the purpose of being sure of seizing upon God. In the past it could be rational, mystical, etc. Today it is sensational and related to consumption. God tends to be an objective satisfaction for us. That is the principal trap in today's piety, for our piety has changed its character. The danger is not necessarily that God should be objectified, in an objective theology like Barth's, for example, but that he should be an object of piety, no longer the active object, but subjected, to the contrary, to our intellectual or spiritual satisfactions.

Finally, prayer can display a quality of acquisition, which also is related to consumption. We talk of *having* faith, of *having* the Holy Spirit, not of living in and by faith, of receiving and being sent forth by the Holy Spirit. We are automatically oriented by our society in this direction of appropriation.

If prayer is to be genuine, it presupposes an inward battle against the promptings of the world, which denature the relationship with God, and hence denature prayer. Thus there must be a "prayer before prayer." The initial action must be an expurgation of that invading power which has shaped me. But obedience to the commandment is going to transform me (Romans 12:1-2). So it even begins as a combat and a calling into question of myself in my acquired instincts. We must accept the fact that prayer can give direction, that it can transform life, but that it never gives a profit, an acquisition. It is never a consumer satisfaction.

That is already taught us by the Lord's Prayer, which

is given to us as a model because it is totally different from "spontaneous" prayer, which springs from the heart of man. It is the opposite to talkativeness, to careless words (Matthew 12:36-37), and to uncertain, inappropriate words centered on our own needs (Matthew 6:7). The "Our Father" is both restrained and disciplined, but especially it is not an expression of our needs. Jesus says explicitly, "Do not be like them [the Gentiles who make many petitions], for your Father knows what you need before you ask him" (Matthew 6:8). Hence it is futile to dissolve into numerous laments before God over what we suppose to be our needs. Either they really are, in which case God knows it, loves us, and supplies our needs, or they are merely misleading advertising images projected by our consumer society. With that put to one side, "Pray *then* like this. . . ."

We can say that the model furnished by Jesus is the anti-consumer prayer par excellence. It is centered on God's needs, not ours. It requires that we realize that God has need that his name be hallowed by the entire creation, and that his will be freely obeyed, loved, and carried out by man. God needs this expression of the love, the trust, and the loyalty of man, such as that of the petition presented by his creature for the coming of the kingdom, for victory over Satan, and for a promise of pardon. But to perform this about-face one must engage in a combat against the self, in and through prayer.

The Achievement of Religionlessness

Prayer is seen immediately to be a warfare along the front of "the religious." I would be out of fashion if I did not speak of "the religious"! Yet behind the fashion there is indeed some truth. Here the difficulty is caused by the fact that prayer has always belonged to religious forms. It is a religious activity. It has always been a part of organized religions. Now, in the revelation of the God of Jesus Christ, it becomes a weapon of warfare against the religious. We know that many of Bonhoeffer's followers are shocked by the fact that in his description of nonreligious Christianity, Bonhoeffer should have retained such a generous place for prayer. Some of them think that this represents his own residual pietism.

To me it appears that the true root of prayer as warfare goes much deeper. We know how first-generation Christianity took concepts, rites, and interpretations of Gnosticism, Stoicism, etc., and transformed them into something quite different by including them within the revelation. These borrowings often turned into their own opposites. The fact that prayer is a religious act is no reason for excluding it from nonreligious Christianity. But we need to make a detour.

I hear very frequent reference to this nonreligious Christianity.* I see nothing original. It is possible to speak of the

* I am not referring here to the "God-is-dead theologies." If the God of Jesus Christ, as such, is dead, nonexistent, or has become nonexistent, it is certain that one can no longer speak of prayer. But neither can one speak of faith or of Christ. It is wholly futile to wrack one's brains trying to explain atheistic Christianity. The only responsible stand to take is to do away with Christianity. Hamilton and Altizer have only to work at philosophy, or politics, or social action. Why do they bother to speak of Christianity? What they are interested in is the world. They fail to realize that their attitude is only a pseudo-radicalism, for it is a radicalism with respect to God. With respect to society it is nothing but a servile conformism.

rejection of worship, of the liturgy, or of hymns. I do see the nonreligious element, but only as a negative, a "privitive." The same is true for the elimination of preaching. I find it hard to see what we have here of a "Christianity," and I have not come upon any valid attempt at morality (for Bonhoeffer's *Ethics* antedates his formulation of nonreligious Christianity). The truth is that what we have here is still an attitude of conformity, more or less, to the desires and wishes of the society of our own day. There is no positive and concrete sign of this nonreligious Christianity. It is a matter of a theological or philosophical dissertation, having nonreligious Christianity as its thesis. We fail to get past the oral stage. The annihilation of the religious within Christianity is not a matter of dissertation, of an intellectual game, nor merely of the elimination of certain forms.

Only a "dereligified" religious act can effectively destroy the religious, for it is not human efficacy or an operation of the intellect that "dereligifies" and desacralizes. It is the effectual, immediate presence of the Living One, of the Wholly Other, of the Transcendent (with all the reservations which those words call for when applied to the One whom nothing can define).

If man is left to his own resources, and acts according to his own designs, he will necessarily reconstruct a religion. The latter can only be displaced by that which is contrary to religion, namely, revelation and grace, that is to say, the Presence. It is the breaking forth of an epiphany which does away with the religious. But we can have no influence whatsoever on that revelation, on that independent, autonomous act. God is the One who decides the how and the when. We have no guarantee, no certainty.* If God is present, and reveals himself as such, then the forms, thoughts, researches, and pieties cease to be religious, for their only purpose is to establish a link with this elusive Unknowable. But it is beyond our power to do that. If we leave it there it is indeed impossible to live a nonreligious Christianity and to combat religion.

But at that point another (and yet the same) way is opened to us, another possibility (and yet the same). This very God has given me a commandment to pray. His incarnation is *also* the nearness which he establishes with each one of us so that we join him in prayer. It is a placing of something at my disposal. God puts himself on my level, so that my prayer may be received by him. He has made himself available to me. Now the act of prayer is returned to my initiative. It takes place if and when I really want it to. It is a "religious" act, belonging to religion, but it is transformed by this *true* rapport with the One who does away with the religious. To the extent to which it is a dereligified religious act, it attacks the religious in its own territory, not outwardly and ineffectually as in a theological discourse, but at the very heart.

Prayer to the God of Jesus Christ is the action par excel-

* What I always find very striking in such writings as those of Bultmann and Bonhoeffer is that God has once again become a passive object, in spite of the claims of these authors who are writing precisely to do battle against "God as object." One manipulates him according to the need of the moment. He is of a piece with the system, just as in classical theology, and nothing is allowed which might call the system into question. There is an "absence of definition," which is in fact a worse way to mummify God than all the dogmas.

lence which annihilates the religious edifice. That edifice cannot be destroyed *except* by the effectual relationship with the living God. That relationship, furthermore, cannot be carried out on our initiative except in obedience to a commandment, which commands us and at the same time makes it possible for us to establish the relationship ourselves. The commandment is that of prayer. Hence prayer is the sole act left to our decision which can attack effectively (not necessarily, of course; there are all the mistakes concerning prayer itself, of which we have spoken) the religion in man's heart, the established, organized religions, and can erect nonreligious Christianity through the relationship (faith and grace) with the Wholly Other. Apart from that it is all literature.

The Only Weapon Against Falsehood

The age of abandonment is also that of great temptations and of great heresies. The two go together. Jesus has forewarned us. The disorders and calamities of the world are but the outer face of the attack directed at turning us away from the Lord. It includes the acclaiming of other lords, and the temptation to despair. The powers of the world especially are at work. There will be devious statements of revelation, and the conflict of the princes of this world grows intense. Prayer is the only weapon for this warfare.

It surely is not possible indiscriminately to let every statement on the subject of revelation go uncriticized. What is heresy is heresy. I am indeed aware of the difficulty. It can be asked, heresy in relation to what? To set up an orthodoxy is itself treason against the Lord, who is precisely the living God intolerant of any rigidity. Moreover, what is heresy for one is not heresy for another. Who is to decide? What is heresy in one epoch is not heresy in another. So in this radical relativism we are tempted to give up treating anything as heresy. We are tempted to let everything pass.

Yet this "liberalism" is a falsehood and a cowardice. There is *one* truth, which we perhaps cannot express or grasp, but which is one.* Falsehood is not truth. Heresy is a falsehood. But at the same time, in the face of this heresy (which is always in good faith, since it is an expression of the activity of the Evil One), forceful, institutional repression, the Catholic policy, is not to the point. Nor is apologetic argument to the point. The repressive attempt is incongruous, since the problem is one of conviction and truth. The apologetic attempt is incongruous because the problem is spiritual and not intellectual.

The only weapon against heresy is prayer. On the one hand, a discernment of spirits is necessary, but that is never a magic practice or a clairvoyance. The discernment of spirits can be accomplished only through prayer, which is a fruit of the presence of the Holy Spirit. On the other hand, once the discernment has been received and the direction and importance of the heresy have been understood, the means of combating it is not one of power, nor of repression or censure or prohibition, but of distinguishing its spiritual origin. This latter is the work of spiritual powers, hence it is on that level only that the battle can be joined. The strength for such a battle is prayer.

That is why Paul (Ephesians 6), after having spoken pre-

---

* It is false to say, as does one death-of-God theologian, that no reply is given in the Gospel to the question, "What is truth?"

cisely of this combat, enumerates all the weapons which we know so well (all of them defensive except one), concluding the list with "prayer." Right after stating that the word of God is the sword of the Spirit, he says, "Pray at all times in the Spirit, with all prayer and supplication." Thus the weapon par excellence is provided by the Spirit. It is the word of God, but the battle can be fought only through prayer. Prayer is the great, open possibility that the truth of Jesus Christ might be received and known. All the other means only produce illusion and religion. Hence we have no guarantee or assurance whereby we can know whether the powers are vanquished, whether heresy is dead, or whether falsehood is done away with. Prayer, our only weapon, does not allow us to survey or chart the territory conquered. Happily, in this warfare there is no victory bulletin. We are asked only to believe that the Lord has chosen this path, and from then on to pray *without ceasing*.

While we are applying prayer in the warfare against religion or against heresy, against the spiritual powers, prayer is acting upon ourselves, without our having to be preoccupied with that aspect or having to make ourselves the object of our prayer. It becomes a life-giving power. If we remain obsessed with ourselves in prayer we make it sterile. If, on the other hand, we are caught up in this warfare of the Lord, it works our own transformation. "He who prays lives, and he who lives prays" (A. Dumas). Living must be understood not only in the spiritual sense, but fully and wholly, in every sense, bodily, in the senses, socially, politically, intellectually *and* spiritually. One does not go without the other. Such is the work of prayer when we allow ourselves to be fully committed to it. There is a combat against myself, to constrain me to pray when nothing else in the world brings me to it.

Finally, when we think of combat, we think of "combat against evil"; and that is indeed true, for we share in the trial that Jesus went through. If he brought off the victory, still we do not get off scot-free. We are united in the death and resurrection of the Lord, through baptism and the Eucharist. The situation of "the pascal tension" throws the baptized person into the mystery of Jesus' testing. We are engaged in his combat, and prayer is our only known resource.

Yet it is important to note that it is precisely Jesus who teaches us a prayer for avoiding that final combat. "Do not make us undergo the test." Granted that we are subject to it, that we have to fight the powers, yet let it not be the final test, that of the absolute temptation, when we think heaven is empty. May we never have to experience the "Why hast thou forsaken me?" May we never be far from thy countenance. May we not be without thee in those last days when, as thou hast said, "no human being would be saved." May that trial not come from thee. Thus the combat in the world against the powers, that combat which is my testing, is at the same time a combat with God, to make him remain with us, that the incarnation should in very truth be constantly renewed.

As Combat Against God

Israel, God's combatant, or he who wrestled with God—such is the name which everyone who prays should bear, for prayer is a striving with God. If we ponder the extreme difficulty of praying in which we find ourselves today, we see that it indicates very directly that prayer, the fruit of conviction, must lay hold upon God to constrain him to "give us his blessing." Prayer cannot be the listing of benefactions which we expect from an obvious and all-powerful intervention. It must be a demand with respect to the hidden God that he reveal himself, that he declare himself and enter into our situation.

It is futile to say that since he is incarnate in Jesus Christ he has become visible, tangible, and near to us. That leads to the idea that there is nothing except the visage of the human Jesus. Make no mistake, we are not in that case stating a new theological position. We are going back to a well-known position derived from Feuerbach, and we have a choice between Jesus who is near because we find him in every man, especially the poor, and Jesus the historical character. Then our faith either is a memorial or is reduced to a morality, in which Jesus is a perfect model whose example we are following.

All that has been tried out a long time ago, and the experiment has shown the sterility of both those positions. They lead very quickly to lukewarmness, to indifference, and to the dismembering of the revelation in Christ. All extreme humanizing of "Christianity" results in its dismemberment, since it is at that point that it no longer means anything.

The Incognito of God

If, therefore, we continue to acknowledge that Jesus is not a mere man, and that his title of Son of man is the dialectical counterpart of the Son of God, then we are confronted with the revealed Incognito of God, or with the incarnation, which reveals, yet at the same time conceals, the Lord. It is out of this Incognito that God gives us the commandment to pray, and each time we obey there is the necessary attempt to uncover him. We require of this God that he reveal himself for what he is, at that moment in which we are praying.

Especially in this time of abandonment we try through prayer to oblige God to turn his face our way once more, to act as God, instead of leaving mankind to flounder in its fog and in its night. We demand both that the creative act be performed in our day, and that this inaugurate the new creation. We cannot be content with a revelation which took place once for all in Jesus Christ, nor with the objectivity of a God who is no longer tangible or present to us. In fact we are looking to see whence our help is to come, but though we are familiar with the answer in the psalm, we demand through prayer that the answer be not theoretical and general, but that it be the contemporary answer of God's decision finally received.

Thus prayer is this striving with the One who is unknowable, beyond our grasp, unapproachable and inexpressible, asking that he finally be, *hic et nunc,* the One he promised he would be. It is a combat, and not the utilization of an object placed at our disposal. It is a combat to open and to pursue the dialogue. We said above that God has laid down the first word of this dialogue. That is true. It is because he began to speak that what follows is possible. Yet the first act is objective. The word is spoken, but has become Scripture. The commandment is addressed to every person, in all ages. I have grasped this commandment, and what I want is the act for today, for this age, and for these persons whom I represent when I speak, and for myself. The God who spoke must speak again. He can no longer leave man to turn in his own individual and collective circle. Prayer is this demand that God not keep silence.

God does keep silence, so prayer maintains the dialogue in spite of all appearances, in the face of every experience. It cannot let God alone. It must be the persistence of that person who goes to his neighbor at midnight asking for bread, and who importunes him until he finally gets out of bed. It must be the persistence of that woman who demands justice of the indifferent judge. That is to say, it is truly a striving with God, of whom one makes demands, whom one importunes, whom one attacks constantly, whose silence and absence one would penetrate at all costs. It is a combat to oblige God to respond, to reveal himself anew.

Prayer is the reverse of the theology of the death of God. The latter starts off with that death as an accomplished fact, and ratifies it by objectifying it. The person who prays, on the other hand, *knows* perhaps that "God is dead," but cannot *accept* it. The Lord's Prayer, in its simplicity, is the very model of that prayer of combat which causes God to "come down" to earth. For the most powerful weapon is that Jesus has taught us to call him Father.

It is a vain, pseudo-scientific pretension on the part of those who rely solemnly on Freud when they denounce "the castrating father," the father oppressor, who is both "the rival of my autonomy and at the same time the guarantor of my desire," toward whom I can have only an Oedipus complex. What a horrible Freudian fantasy, which makes us think that in calling upon the Father we are only making a show of submission, when we would really love to seize for ourselves the attributes we are ascribing to the Father, with the idea of supplanting him. Or again, it supposes that in resorting to prayer we are being infantile and afraid to assume our responsibilities as persons.

The vision of the Father which Jesus gives us is quite different from that, and the same applies to our sonship. Yet it is also a warning that "God is a father in a way in which fathers are not usually fathers" (Crespy). Thus, in praying to this Father in conformity with the Bible, we are bearing witness to the fact that "God is not the Father in the way in which, humanly, we believe simply that he is the father, because too often we believe him to be that in the same way in which we have tried to be gods, that is to say, by giving in to desire. God is not God in the same way in which man has wanted to be God" (Mottu). You who are only men, will you give evil things to your children? Is there something bourgeois or backward in the knowledge that there is also such a thing as love which is true, simple, pure, authentic, a love of reciprocal giving, of unambiguous trust, a love which gives itself, a love of knowledge and fullness between a father and his children, profitable for the one as for the others?

To call God our Father is first of all to cleanse the father-child relationship of all the alienation which Freudianism has discovered, or thinks it has discovered. It is to confess openly (precisely because it is the Father to whom I am praying), not that I give up the Father, but that I give up being myself the father, that is, I give up taking myself for God. Yet it is also, and at the same time, to act upon God. It is to lay hold upon him in such a way that he can no longer keep silence and remain detached. I find so much truth in Péguy's excellent poem "The Mystery of the Holy Innocents":

(God speaks)

> "*Our Father who art in heaven,* he knew what he was doing
> That day, my Son who loved them so,
> Who lived in their midst, who was as one of them,
> Who went about as they did, who talked with them,
> who lived as they lived,
> Who suffered as they suffered, who died as they died.
>
> He knew very well what he was doing that day, my Son
> who loved them so,
> When he placed that barrier between them and me, *Our Father*
> *Who art in heaven,* those three or four words,
> That barrier which my anger and perhaps my justice
> will never cross.
>
> Those three or four words which go ahead like a beautiful
> pointed prow in front of a miserable ship,
> And which cut through the waves of my wrath
> And when the point of the prow has passed, the ship passes,
> and the whole fleet after it.
>
> My Son knew full well what to do
> To bind the arms of my justice and to loose the arms
> of my mercy.

And now I must judge them like a Father.

That is what my Son told them. My Son betrayed to them
        the secret of judgment itself.

Just as the wake of a great ship grows wider and wider,
        until it disappears and is lost
Yet begins with a point, which is the point of the ship itself,
So the tremendous wake of sinners grows wider and wider,
        until it disappears and is lost
Yet begins with a point; and it is that point which is
        coming toward me,
Which is turned toward me.

And the ship is my own Son, laden with all the sins of
        the world,
And the point of the ship: those are my Son's two hands
        joined together.

And that point: those are the three or four words,
        Our Father . . .
And behind, growing wider and wider until it disappears
        and is lost,
Is the wake of the prayers without number
As they are spoken in their text throughout days without
        number
By innumerable men
(By the simple men, his brothers . . .)

This whole fleet of prayers, laden with the sins of the world,
This whole fleet of prayers and of penitence is attacking me

Having the pointed prow that you know.
Coming toward me with the pointed prow that you know
Is a cargo fleet
And a fleet of the line,
A battle fleet,
Like a great fleet of the ancients, like a fleet of triremes
Advancing to attack the King.
And I—what would you have me do? I am being attacked,
And in this fleet, in this innumerable fleet,
Every *Our Father* is like a mighty warship
Which has its own pointed prow, *Our Father* . . .
Turned toward me, and which advances behind its pointed
prow." *

Here is God bound, when we call him Father, with a bond
which nothing can break; and all the modern theories about
God, all the discourses, will never change it.

A Combat of Total Involvement

But God does not yield easily. He does not change with
every wind. He does not give in to just any prayer. It is not
that there are good and bad prayers, some pious, good, and
proper, while others are silly, irrational, and heterodox.
There are only those in which man commits himself from
the depths of his being, wholly and without reserve, and
those other prayers that one "says," which are deeply emo-
tional but with a feeling different from that of Jesus Christ.
There are also ritual and formal prayers. The combat with
God implies the commitment of the person who is praying.

* The translation used here is by C. E. Hopkin.

Here, undoubtedly, we come back to the idea (which we criticized) that the person who prays should carry out what he is demanding! But that is not the initial aspect of the commitment. The second aspect is what is involved, just as to love one's neighbor is the second commandment. The first is the commitment *with, for,* but we must also add *against* God. One cannot hold oneself in reserve, one cannot pretend to be aloof in the venture in which one is asking God to involve himself fully.

Abraham's prayer goes to the very limit of bargaining and argument, even to the point of infringing on God's decision. Jacob's prayer commits all of his strength to the combat: "I will not let you go." What determination, what violence! The kingdom of heaven belongs to the violent who lay hold upon it, and let us not talk about "holy violence." It is an extreme and sacrilegious violence, which is saintly in fact.

But this violence is not accepted by God unless the person practicing it is ready himself to bear the shock in return. If God receives a prayer, the first consequence falls upon the person praying. Abraham had to submit to the sacrifice of his son as an answer to his prayer for Sodom. Jacob's thigh was put out of joint, and he went away lame. However, the most usual experience will be God's decision to put to work the person who cries out to him.

Yet we must be careful. The pattern is not simple. It is not merely, "If I pray for bread for the hungry, I must give them bread," or "I should fight against social injustice," for God's decision is often out of proportion to the prayer, and the answer is not what is hoped for. When Elijah, in the wilderness, demands, "It is enough; now, O Lord, take away my life," God answers, "Arise and eat, else the journey will be too great for you"; then afterward, "Return to this people and begin your work again." Also, when Jonah agrees to pay for his disobedience with his life, God takes him back, to make him do what needs to be done.

Whoever wrestles with God in prayer puts his whole life at stake. Otherwise it would not be a *genuine* combat, or indeed it would not be a combat *with God*. Whence, though prepared to give up his life, he can only accept the decision which sends him elsewhere, wherever God judges best. In the combat in which man has no reservations, God wills also to have no reservations, and if God has already given everything in his Son, then he expects man both to take him with complete seriousness in prayer and also to conduct himself responsibly.

To take him with complete seriousness means to put him to the test. We never dare enough in petitioning God, in putting him to the test of what he can do (and of what he has already wanted to do, since we have the promise). It is not resorting to magic or uncivilized to demand something of God, as when Elijah asked that the sacrificial victims be burned, or when Jesus asked that the fruitless fig tree wither. It is, rather, the audacity of knowing that God can do that, and of committing oneself to asking him. It is a commitment of the self, because what a blow it is if God remains silent! What doubt and what ridicule can result! If our prayers are prudent and empty, that is because we have become incapable of putting God to the test. We are afraid of risking our reputations. We are anxious about spiritual things, in which we can never be certain of being answered or denied, and we are anxious about good theology (the good being the latest). We treat the demand for a miracle as the mark of a backward, materialistic mind, etc.

In fact, we are afraid, both that God might manifest himself and that we might be committed unreservedly and without limit. That is the last observation to be made. Whoever enters into combat with God should be aware of the fact that once it is begun it can never be brought to a halt. It has to be pursued to the very end. If a person does not have the courage to go the limit, it is best in that case to stay with the prudent and untroubled request, which has no importance and which guarantees psychological tranquillity. The warnings which Jesus gives us apply as well to prayer. To engage in prayer is to perform the basic act of a disciple, and at that moment one is radically alone before God. One finds oneself separated from those nearest him, at the same time that he is in communion with them. That is the fulfillment of the saying, "Every one who has left houses or brothers or sisters or father or mother or children or lands, for my name's sake, will receive a hundredfold." That renunciation is required for the disciple's independence and for the seriousness of prayer (Luke 14: 25-33).

So it is important to know whether one is ready to go all the way in the combat and the commitment. God does not tolerate lukewarmness. We must know that genuine prayer is infinitely simple and radically serious. We need to sit down first and count the cost, to see whether we can complete the tower, whether the army at our disposal (the "Our Father") is sufficient for the battle. It is impossible to take prayer lightly, for there is where we meet the radicalism of faith.

As long as we are not engaged in the combat of prayer, our radicalism is necessarily a discourse; and unfortunately, a discourse about God, or about man, or about the absence of God, or about our society has nothing radical in it. The radical begins where man takes God by force, where God himself is present. Radicalism is not *really* produced by some procedure of the intellect, or of the will to action, whatever it might be. It is brought about by the presence of God alone. The whole Bible, from beginning to end, attests that. It even constitutes, in all probability, the central theme of the kerygma.

Prayer is the precise point at which this radicalism is brought about in the unhindered meeting between God and man. That is why it is a decisive combat and a final commitment. Such is the measure of the seriousness of the combat against God, to constrain him to become the Father once again, in this age in which he has turned the other way.

THE ACT OF HOPE

Just as the second commandment is irrevocably tied to the first, and is likened to it, so in prayer the commitment on behalf of man is decisively bound to the commitment with God. If a person thinks of prayer as a way of not getting involved, of not acting, of avoiding risk, if he supposes that prayer lets him escape fatigue and danger, assures him of tranquillity and a good conscience, gives him all-around protection, then we can say not only that he has not understood the reality of prayer, but also that he is stepping into the most dangerous enterprise of all, for that is the point of the prophecy of Amos (5:18-20), "Woe to you who desire the day of the Lord! . . ."

But when we speak of commitment on behalf of man, we are not thinking necessarily of political involvement, or of social reform, or of revolution. That is not impossible, but in spite of our current obsession with politics and social justice, it is not the most important feature. As a by-product, on occasion, for this or that person, that path is good, but it is not the truth and the life. To the contrary, it is sometimes falsehood and death.

We must not forget that the combat on behalf of man is surprisingly characterized by Paul (I Timothy 2:1-4) as a "prayer for the salvation of all men," for God desires all men to be saved, and also as a prayer for the civil authorities, because we depend on them for being able to lead a "possible" life. So this initial aspect is a combat for the salvation of all. The prayer for all mankind corresponds to the will for the salvation of all. But that implies a commitment, without reservations, to the sacerdotal function. In prayer we participate in the mediatorial office. In that prayer we represent the whole people which God has ransomed. Hence prayer cannot help being universal (without being abstract), but that is true only when it is a combat, not when it is a monotonous repetition.

It is a combat on behalf of men, but also, if need be, against them, insofar as this prayer involves the proclamation of the truth to the indifferent person. It is to this extent that there is no frontier between the Church and the world. The prayer for all men attests this difficult relation of love, which both gives of itself and makes demands. Prayer which rests on that faith and on that love for all men is in no way the expression of a vague and generalized humanitarianism. It is the commitment, without reservation, of all our strength to the single point of the salvation won for all in Jesus Christ. Apart from that, prayer is meaningless.

One can see that all the facets of the combat hang together, the struggle against my own feelings, against the indifference of others, against the incognito of God, all of which is made necessary by the fact that we must pray for all mankind. But we must pray also for the civil authorities. There again, I have to fight against myself (my servility toward the authorities, or, on the other hand, my critical and rebellious attitude), and against the authorities themselves (if I pray for them I should demand that they really carry out their functions) and against the seeming indifference of God in politics.

Yet in praying for the civil authorities, while committed to the hilt, I nevertheless need to realize that I can only expect from them something very relative. The unusual passage from Paul is basic. We are to pray "for kings, and all who are in high positions, that we may lead a quiet and peaceable life." So I am not to look for justice, or truth, or freedom, or "the solution," etc., but for a quite relative situation of tranquillity. "Life," in this passage, is the Greek word *bios* (physical life), not *zoe*. I am not to expect a spiritual life from the authorities, but simply the minimum of order, independence, and stability, so that human life may be physically possible. It is quite relative, and yet very important. Without it nothing else can come about.

So there we are held to a deep commitment in order to

obtain something quite relative, and beneficial to that very relative world, society. We know that the image of this world is passing and is consigned to dust. Yet God commands us to pray without ceasing for this lowly dwelling place of earth, that it may be habitable, but also that it remain *humble,* and that we may not be tempted to exalt it as though it were the kingdom of God.

Prayer for society puts the latter in its place. In spite of all its strength and technical successes, its scientific excellence and its "great society," it is a poor little commonplace, transitory reality, for which it is absolutely necessary to pray. Without that persistent prayer, this grandiose society will soon be nothing but a frenzy of pride and suicide. Without the intercession of the saints, its history will be nothing but "a tale told by an idiot." But the moment social action is based on this prayer, then that action can take on a lively versatility. Prayer makes complete sense, both in terms of resistance to fate and folly, and at the same time in terms of obedience and loyalty; both as a clearing away of falsehood, a bringing down of human pretensions, and at the same time as a listening-post for the hope and the stammering of this same human being.

The Ultimate Act

Since it rests upon the promise of God, prayer is the ultimate act of hope, otherwise it has no substance. Because it is an act of hope, every prayer is necessarily eschatological. There is not one prayer for the present and another for the future. There is not a hope which is made tangible in terms of an answer to a present problem, and another hope for the end of time. There is not a prayer of petition for today and a prayer of petition for later on. God's today is the end of the ages. "Today you will be with me in Paradise," replies Jesus to the crucified criminal who prays to him. If your prayer is answered (but how, you do not know), it is because you have entered into the kingdom of God, today, not by your eventful present, but by the very presence of the Lord of the ages.

Prayer is both the action which plants us in that end of the age, at the coming of the kingdom, and it is also the action which causes the kingdom to come. Just as all prayer begins with "Our Father," so it should also conclude with "Come, Lord Jesus." The field of force of prayer is exerted between those two poles. One does not go without the other. The current of the present is there. Thus prayer is given its meaning. If you pray, that means that those last days which are coming are present when you pray. You are making present what is promised for the new creation. Eschatology is realized through this specific relationship with God, not, to be sure, in an objective and universally perceptible manner. God carries out his decision in hearing and in responding to the prayer of those who cry to him, "How long?" (Revelation 6:10). The coming of the new creation does not require a preparation of man, but an agreement between him who decides and him who appeals. God is not arbitrary, and even for the final creation he acts in the relationship of love with his creature, who expresses himself in prayer.

This relation between the end of the age and prayer is constantly indicated, either by the fact that prayer brings the end nearer or that it prepares the way for it. "The end of all things is at hand; therefore keep sane and sober for your prayers" (I Peter 4: 7). But let us beware of a misunderstanding. This passage does not refer necessarily to the negative aspect of the coming. The end is also the goal, the fulfillment. It is not a matter merely of the unfolding of history, or of a threat (the end of the world), but *also* of the fact everything has reached its objective, which is also its fulfillment.

It is both a fulfillment of what we human beings have wished for, hoped for, and striven for in our history, and a fulfillment of what God had willed, hoped for, and chosen. Hence, to speak of this "coming" does not mean, "the world will soon come to an end" but, rather, "the kingdom of God has come near to you, it is within you, it is in your midst," which corresponds to the great affirmation, "It is finished." There is not some goal to be reached in a more or less distant future. The goal is already attained.

But if we understand the beginning of the passage in this way, we must guard against the habitual misinterpretation of the statement "therefore be sane and sober." Especially should we not understand it to mean "because the end of the world is near, since everything will disappear, you can be detached from all that is about to perish, in order to devote yourself to prayer" or, what is worse, "since death is at hand, along with the judgment of God, let us hasten to pray, in order to put ourselves right with him." These are abominable heresies and blasphemies. They represent a sinister distrust of the Father.

Our text is saying to us, "Since it is finished, since all is attaining its goal, you can live already as people who are in the kingdom, and you should do so." Now the first step in this life in the kingdom is that of wisdom and prayer. "Be sane and sober," that is to say, learn to discern the truth in which you are already living. Discern the truth of things and the truth of lives, of situations and of events. That implies a knowledge of the provisional and relative character of everything you do, of all that exists, yet of its indispensable and valid character at the same time. It implies a knowledge of the assured reality of the flowering, of the arrival at the goal, yet of its secret character also, reserved as it is for faith, for the time being.

This is the very setting of the life of prayer. It is part and parcel of daily living, yet it is a request for the completion of the work of God, for its ultimate fulfillment. Only in prayer involved in (not detached from) the actual situation can we live concretely the life of the end of the age, and share in the presence of the kingdom. The continuation of the biblical passage in question is very demanding. With this prayer as a starting point, life is to be lived with "an unfailing love." Thus eschatological prayer necessarily brings us back to the life of current events, but for quite another purpose than merely to take part in these events.

Prayer and Social Participation

Total involvement in prayer demands of us a participation in society, in the lives of those close to us, of those at a distance, of intimate friends, and of strangers. Prayer has no limits. If it cannot be abstract it is (in contrast to agape) possible for large bodies of people, for those we do not know, precisely to the extent to which its substance and meaning come from God. But if prayer does not dispense from action, if it is the opposite to "rejection of the world," if it must relate constantly to events (and not lose itself in mystical, vague, and diffuse effusions), we still find it hard to believe today that prayer is more important than action.

It is indeed true that the content of prayer should be supplied by the world (in which our action is to be manifested), and that it is vain to pray abstractly. That is to say that normally our prayer should be generated by concrete situations, and that in the degree in which it is linked with action, it involves specific concern. It is useless to pray for peace or for justice, unless one is specific about what peace or what justice. Prayer must involve the courage of unilateral action, a courage of which the Reformers gave proof when, after the example of the Psalmists and of Scripture, they did not hesitate to curse their enemies, according to Mottu.

Yet, however important this active viewpoint may be, it is prayer which dominates. With respect to the world, prayer is the act of bringing reality into the presence of God (Ebeling). We agree spontaneously to action, and then to add prayer to it, but the order is the reverse of that, namely, to pray, and then to act because of having prayed, as a function of that prayer. Of course, on behalf of action (on behalf of the practical), one can say that action alone is of any use. It is the only thing which does not lie. Its failures or successes are out in the open. It alone corresponds to human need today, hence to the second commandment. Finally, the present-day world* is not made for contemplation. But

---

* One often adds at this point, "in contrast to the Middle Ages," but what a misapprehension concerning the Middle Ages—as though that harsh epoch of disorders, of popular uprisings and wars were a sort of age of contemplation! It took a lot of determination to lead a life of prayer in a society far more tumultuous than ours.

in all that, we are faced, on the one hand, with the activist ideology and, on the other hand, with a complete ignorance of the combat of prayer.

Prayer goes with action, but it is prayer which is radical and decisive. Every action will necessarily be taken over by the milieu in which it occurs. It will be turned aside from its purpose. It will be vitiated by circumstances. It will entail unforeseeable consequences and will drag misfortune in its train. Prayer, on the other hand, when it is genuine, cannot be taken over (since it obtains its import and substance from God). It attains its goal. It entails the consequences granted by God.

Action really receives its character from prayer. Prayer is what attests the finitude of action and frees it from its dramatic or tragic aspect. Since it shows that the action is not final, it brings to it humor and reserve. Otherwise we would be tempted to take it with dreadful seriousness. But in so doing prayer bestows upon action its greatest authenticity. It rescues action from activism, and it rescues the individual from bewilderment and despair in his action. It prevents his being engulfed in panic when his action fails, and from being drawn into activism, when he is incited to more and more activity in pursuit of success, to the point of losing himself. Prayer, because it is the warrant, the expression of my finitude, always teaches me that I must *be more* than my action, that I must live with my action, and even that my action must be lived with by another in *his* action. Thanks to prayer, I can see that truth about myself and my action, in hope and not in despair.

In this combat, the Christian who prays acts more effectively and more decisively on society than the person who is politically involved, with all the sincerity of his faith put into the involvement. It is not a matter of seeing them in opposition to one another, but of inverting our instinctive, cultural hierarchy of values. The action is not the test of prayer, nor is it the proof of its importance or the measure of its genuineness. It is prayer which is the qualifying factor, the significance, the foundation of the truth of the action.

Apart from prayer, action is necessarily violence and falsehood. Even technological action, in spite of its appearance of neutrality and objectivity, is nevertheless in that category. Prayer is the only possible substitute for violence in human relations. Henceforth it is from prayer that one expects action to take its value. Action is no longer looked to for the immediate, visible, and expected result at any cost. Prayer guarantees the objective (perhaps unexpected) of action, but by that very fact it cannot tolerate every action. This is in contrast to what was done in the Inquisition (Pray for the salvation of the heretics, and burn them), or recommended by the Church in France in 1939 (Pray for the enemy, but kill him). It goes without saying that this use of prayer is blasphemous. It is impossible to engage in the combat of prayer for the brother whom one loves in Christ, and still to employ physical and psychological violence against him.

Thus prayer calls violence to account as a value, as an ultimate argument, as a means to be taken for granted. If we choose to use violence, so be it, but in that case let us stop playing the farce of prayer and love of neighbor. It is a decision one has to make. But we must be honest, and in so acting we should know (yet when we have chosen violence, we are no longer capable of knowing) that we are losing our best chance of success and our contact with truth. We should know, also, that our position is in the end far less radical, for in choosing violence we are participating completely in a world of violence, in a society in which violence reigns at every level and in all forms, in the ideology of the practical and of violence. As violent persons, we are fully conformed to the world. Violence is one of the "rudiments" (*stoicheia*) of this world.

Prayer, by contrast, is a much more radical break, a more fundamental protest. In that decision, in that combat, the world can have no part, since we have a share in the prayer, the sacrifice, and the resurrection of the one Jesus Christ. All further radicalism, of behavior, of style of life and of action, can only have the prior rupture of prayer as its source. Precisely because our technological society is given over entirely to action, the person who retires to his room to pray is the true radical. Everything will flow from that. This act in society, which is also an action on this society, goes very much further than the concrete involvement, which it still does not shirk.

Prayer, in the degree in which it is the decision we have described, addressed to the One who issued the call in the first place, the Wholly Other and at the same time the Transcendent, is in reality the exact counterpoint of the rigorous mechanism of the technological society. It is the path which makes it possible to transform man's objectification and alienation. It is true independence with respect to the unfailing omnipotence of the state. It is a true nonconformity toward psychological ideologies and manipulations. It is all that in truth, in contrast to action which is called revolutionary, and which today is a pure illusion, a flight from the inexorable, a dream of a better day which is never to be.

Prayer is flexibility within organizational rigidity. It is a positive challenge to the individualist-collectivist dilemma. Finally, it is the commitment which balances the fever for consumer goods and the obsession with efficacy. It is the sole necessary and sufficient action and practice, in a society which has lost its way.

Prayer and History

Because it is eschatological and radical, it is prayer which makes history, but it does not do this alone. The book of Revelation, in giving us an image of the forces which constitute history, describes the four horses: war and the power of the state, famine and economic power, sickness and the intuition of death, and then the white horse who went out conquering and to conquer, which is the word of God (Revelation 6: 1ff.).

So, among the powers let loose on earth, it is the word of God, intermingled with the others, which makes history, but it alone is victorious. It is the one which finally guarantees that the history of mankind is not all disaster and annihilation. It is a presence on earth, in the midst of men, *within* history, of that word. So the Word Incarnate, with its sequel of sacrament, the proclamation of the message and prayer—those are the current aspects of the incarnation. If one of the three is lacking, the incarnation is not present, which means that history is not being made.

We might accumulate activities, revolutions, institutions, epics, massacres, production, and culture, and what would come out of it would not be history but a confused mixture of misfortune and surfeit. If Christ is not in this age, still incarnate in it, then that is all there is to the history of our time, the history which we are called upon to produce. There is neither beginning, nor focal point, nor conclusion. The alpha and omega are missing from our vision and understanding, for, by means of a disincarnate faith, we put these off onto an eternity which is unrelated to history.

Of these three ongoing actions of the incarnation, which are both individual and communal, it is prayer which constitutes the meeting place between God's word and the human word, under the form of a dialogue. It is inseparable from the other two. It associates us with the hidden work of the word. (And here the great passage from Pascal takes on its full import once again; but it is not so much a mechanical or a philosophical causality which is given by God to man. It is a historical causality.) It associates us with God's design in history.

This present incarnation is both the way and the structure of our history. If the way is known to God, the structure has constantly to be put together and assured by us. What is decisive is not the tension between a future eschatology and a realized eschatology. It is, rather, the movement of the Christ who comes to us. That is translated by the introduction on our part of the eschatological kingdom into the today of God's design. But our action in this connection is only, and can only be, prayer itself.

Thus the act of private prayer is the act through which history is structured in Christ, and it is at this point that the transition from "I" to "We" is inevitable. There is no room for opposition between private, individual prayer and communal, churchly prayer (which is too readily confused with *group* prayer). The most private, informal, and personal of prayers (if indeed we are dealing really with prayer) is necessarily a prayer on behalf of all, since by that act (even if the person praying has no such conscious intention and makes no mention of politics) the history of all takes on meaning and possibility for the future.

Then prayer has its full measure, for we are placed in the midst of the ultimate combat (which is always present) against "nothingness in action." The ancient biblical image for nothingness (the serpent, leviathan), which is always ready to swallow up, corresponds to a reality, both present and final. Only prayer can bring off the victory, and it depends upon us that this victory take place. "For the person who truly prays, the demonic is a horrible dream of incongruity" (Castelli). That is indeed the essential point. Nothingness at work expresses itself in the impossibility of history, in futility, in incongruity (the transient, the unstable, the irresponsible, the disorganized, the nonmoral, etc.). Prayer gives consistency to life, to action, to human relations, to the facts of human existence, both small and great. Prayer holds together the shattered fragments of the creation. It makes history possible. Therefore it is victory over nothingness.

"The God of peace has willed that one person pray for all, just as in one man he himself has borne all men" (Cyprian, *De domin. orat.,* 8). Let us note well that sacrament and preaching lose their import and reality if prayer does not accompany them.

Such is the ultimate meaning of the combat of prayer, in which we discover that obedience in the face of every natural inclination and hope in the face of every probability take on a value far surpassing our personal concerns. At every moment the eschatological act of prayer is a combat against death and nothingness, so that we may pick up once again the thread of life.